THE FUTURE GLORY

THE FUTURE GLORY

GLORY

The Charismatic Renewal
and the Implementation of Vatican II

Joseph Bagiackas

Charismatic Renewal Services

Scripture quotations are from the Revised Standard Version unless otherwise indicated.

Published by: Charismatic Renewal Services, Inc.
237 N. Michigan St.
South Bend, Indiana 46601

Printed in the United States of America.
Library of Congress Card Catalog Number: 83-070962
ISBN 0-943780-02-0

Cover design by Cae Carnick
Cover drawing by Franklin McMahon (detail)

This drawing was made during the opening days of Vatican Council II. Franklin McMahon was in Rome often during the course of the council and his drawings and paintings were widely published. His new book, *This Church, These Times,* includes works from the council, works concerning Catholics in Japan and India, and the travels of Pope Paul VI and of Pope John Paul II to Mexico, Poland and the United States.

First printing

. . . my Spirit continues in your midst; do not fear! For thus says the Lord of hosts: One moment yet, a little while, and I will shake the heavens and the earth, the sea and the dry land. I will shake all the nations, and the treasures of all the nations will come in, And I will fill this house with glory, says the Lord of hosts. Mine is the silver and mine is the gold, says the Lord of hosts. Greater will be THE FUTURE GLORY of this house than the former, says the Lord of hosts; And in this place I will give you peace, says the Lord of hosts.

Haggai 2:5-9 NAB

"The Spirit of God . . . directs the course of time and renews the face of the earth. . . ."

(*Constitution on the Church in the Modern World*, 26)

CONTENTS:

I would like to thank Fr. Steve Avella, Kerry Koller, Tom Noe, Fr. Dick Korsinek, Paul DeCelles, Kevin Ranaghan and Dan DeCelles, who read all or part of the manuscript and made helpful comments. I especially thank Paul DeCelles for his counsel with regard to sacraments, spirituality and parishes. I also want to thank Tom Noe for his work as copy editor and Margaret Kelly for typing the manuscript.

I gratefully dedicate this book to the bishops of the Second Vatican Council, who, through their courage and vision, have given the church a path into the future.

INTRODUCTION:

The Purpose of This Book

Often we charismatics are asked the following types of questions by Catholics outside the renewal: "How does all this relate to the sacraments?" "Is this part of the new Pentecost of Vatican II?" "Does it lead you into a more mature spiritual life?" "How will it help parishes?" "Doesn't it take away from social-justice concerns?" We even ask these questions among ourselves from time to time. They are good questions, questions which we ought to be able to answer in a way that defends the renewal and shows that it benefits the church. This book will, I hope, enable the reader better to explain, both to outsiders and to other charismatics, the meaning of the charismatic experience and its connection with the renewal of the church.

Each chapter considers a different aspect of the Catholic mentality and tries to show how charismatic life enriches and enhances it. Chapter one offers an interpretation of the vision of Vatican II and shows how the fullness of the Spirit is meant to enable us to implement the council's vision.

1

Chapter two shows how Catholic spiritual life, as it is traditionally viewed, is enlivened and made real through the charismatic experience. The next chapter is a reflection on how a person's sacramental life can be renewed by the release of the Spirit. Chapter four covers the impact of the renewal on parish life and offers some suggestions as to how this aspect of Catholic life can be strengthened through the fostering of charismatic groups. Chapter five deals with a new aspect of the Catholic mentality—evangelism. Charismatics have taken the lead among Catholics in developing new methods for evangelism. The chapter discusses several guidelines for personal witness that have been used by many people in the renewal and have proven over the years to be very fruitful. The sixth chapter shows how life in the Spirit can enrich a person's practice of social justice.

Two aspects of the Catholic mentality that I will not consider in this book are the Catholic scriptural consciousness, which has become much stronger since the council, and Marian piety. Certainly, one major way to explain the renewal is to tell how it restores many scriptural practices to Christian life. Another is to show how it can aid us in understanding the role of Mary. However, many other books have been written on these subjects and, rather than repeating what has already been said in other places, I felt that readers would benefit more if I simply referred them to that literature. There are many books on how the charismatic experience brings scripture to life, but the most helpful treatment on the popular level is Steve Clark's *Baptized in the Spirit and Spiritual Gifts*. With regard to Mary and the renewal, Fr. George Kosicki has written several excellent pieces.

This book is not meant for experts. I have written it from the viewpoint of a Catholic layperson who has been active in the charismatic renewal for many years and is trying to sort out his experience. Knowing that most participants in the renewal try to do the same thing from time to time, I felt that it would be helpful if one of those persons, namely myself, shared about his efforts in a way that those of us who are "rank and file" Catholic charismatics could relate to. Some of what I say in this book has been said more expertly by others. For those who seek a more precise understanding of the topics I will consider, I recommend that they read something more fully developed.

The subtitle of this book is "The Charismatic Renewal and the Implementation of Vatican II." Although only one of the chapters deals directly with the council, the whole book is an attempt to show how life in the Spirit is in harmony with the spirit of Vatican II. The spirit and purpose of the council, as Pope John Paul II has stated, is "the enrichment of faith."* Each chapter analyzes from a different standpoint how the charismatic experience enriches Catholic faith.

I wanted in this book to draw attention to the renewal and its intimate connection with the council for two reasons. First, though the council is often mentioned by charismatic leaders, few charismatics are able to relate their practical daily life in the Spirit to its vision. This book attempts to bridge the gap between the council's vision and its practical application in charismatic life.

Second, there are very few persons, whether progressive, moderate or conservative, who are optimistic with regard to the future of the conciliar agenda. Charismatics are no more hopeful than others. But we *are* hopeful about the power of God at work in the world today. I believe that our optimism about God at work should include hope about the council, because it is a major (if not *the* major) part of the Spirit's work, though we tend not to recognize it as such. One way we can grow in our recognition of how the Spirit is moving powerfully through the council is to see how its aims and vision are the same as those the Lord has given us in the renewal. Much of chapter one is devoted to showing how this is the case.

Chapter seven of this book, entitled "The 12 Rhemas," is an account of how the charismatic renewal has unfolded spiritually over the years. Contrary to the opinions of many who believe that the renewal has peaked and is gradually withering away, I feel that God has been guiding his charismatic people all along, is continuing to guide them, and has a future goal in mind for them. Some say the renewal has

*See Karol Wojtyla (John Paul II), *Sources of Renewal* (San Francisco: Harper & Row, 1980), p.15.

peaked numerically, but there are indications to the contrary. In any event, it has not peaked in terms of the spiritual growth of those who continue in it. The chapter shows how this growth has taken place, what its implications for today are, and where the Lord may be taking us in the future. As the title of the book suggests, I believe that our future, as sons and daughters of God who are born of the Spirit, is one of glory.

Method of Presentation

Although the implementation of Vatican II is a major theme of this book, quotes from the council are not as common as one might expect. I have taken this direction for several reasons. First, many books on the council quote the documents heavily, almost to the point of getting in the way of what the author is trying to say. Also, quoting constantly from the documents can be a distraction for the normal reader. Therefore, in the interests of readability and clarity, I have used them sparingly.

Second, it has been my experience that using the terminology of the documents as a main part of one's presentation—in talks as well as in writing—weighs heavily on the mind of the normal Catholic.

Third, although people in the charismatic movement experience a kind of spiritual renewal which is similar to the one called for by the council, they seldom use the council's terminology to describe their experience. They use scriptural terms, sacramental ideas, concepts drawn from traditional spirituality, and so on. Speaking to peoples' experience and using terminology they are comfortable with and pointing out how this is in harmony with the council seemed the best way to promote a greater love for the council on the part of charismatics.

CHAPTER 1:

Vatican II

To understand the meaning of the charismatic renewal, it is first necessary to see how it fits into what has been happening worldwide in the church in the past 30 years and what is likely to happen in the next generation. What we need is a kind of historical blueprint of the church from 1950 to 2020. What has happened since World War II? What is happening now? What can be said, with some degree of assurance, about what will happen in the next 40 years, assuming the Lord does not come before then? If we can get a vision for this era in the history of the church, and can see how the baptism in the Spirit is affecting this history, we will know better how to proceed in the Spirit.

Before the Council

During the 50s and early 60s, I grew up as a member of a prosperous, postwar, American Catholic parish. During that period, parish membership increased fivefold; a new school and bigger church were built, and Catholicism flourished as

men and women who had been through the war settled
down, raised their children and participated in the steadily
rising level of prosperity in postwar America.

I remember this time as one of real peace and spiritual
stability in my life and in the life of my parish. We were
basically good kids; we were altar boys, Catholic girl scouts
and boy scouts, students at our parish grade school, active
in CYO and so on. We didn't get drunk or high on drugs;
we respected our parents, believed the right things in the
areas of faith and morals, and admiringly looked to the
nuns and priests for spiritual strength and inspiration. Our
parents, as far as we could tell, seemed also to have strong
Catholic lives. They worked hard, sacrificed for us, participated in parish organizations such as the Altar Society,
men's clubs and PTA, and supported the direction and
training given us by the nuns and priests.

The key pieces, religiously speaking, in the life of my
parish were three priests. They said Mass and heard our
confessions dutifully, served as chaplains for the different
parish organizations, and represented the Catholic Church
to groups and organizations outside the church. These men
were our leaders and our models. They were the embodiment of a clear, orderly, unified religious consciousness.

Meanwhile, in Rome and in other centers of Catholic
thought and leadership, popes, bishops and religious thinkers sensed the need for change. Yes, in many respects, the
church was at a high point in her history. There was clarity
and order in the area of authority. There was a good deal of
unity in the area of belief. The church was growing numerically. Churches and seminaries were full in many places.
But there were problems on the horizon. Attitudes of legalism and minimalism were strong in the church. In some
ways, she was becoming more and more out of step with
the modern world. A siege mentality prevailed. There was a
great gulf between laity and clergy. New developments in
the area of scripture studies, patristics and liturgy were
laying bare many of the inadequacies of preconciliar Catholic thought, which had overly emphasized the approach of
textbook scholasticism to church life. The Holy Spirit was
calling for change.

The church responded to the impulse of the Spirit by calling the Second Vatican Council and inaugurating a new era in the history of the church and the world.

The Meaning of Vatican II

It is not easy for a normal Catholic layperson to understand the Second Vatican Council and its implications for Christianity. The documents of the council are 400 pages in length, and some of what they deal with cannot be grasped without theological background. The statements which have come out since the council are no easier to understand, and, when taken together, they are much more lengthy than the documents. The history of the ideas and events which surrounded the council is far more complex than the documents it has produced.

However, a basic understanding of the spirit of Vatican II can be gained by grasping its six general thrusts and the method for its implementation. These interpenetrating thrusts are *aggiornamento* (updating), *back to the sources* (mainly the Bible and the Church Fathers), *the pastoral thrust* (not mainly dogmatic), *participation* (as opposed to spectatorship in the church), *ecumenism* and *dialogue* (as opposed to polemics and a siege mentality). The underlying method to be used in implementing the thrusts of the council is that every *enrichment* of the council must be *integrated* into what was already good in the church before the council.* Only when the complementary processes of enrichment and integration have taken place can an initiative of the council become authentic renewal. Let us now discuss these thrusts and the underlying method for implementation.

Aggiornamento

Aggiornamento is that thrust of the council which examines every area of church life in order to see what can be ad-

justed and brought more into harmony with the pulse of
modern life, without taking away from what is good and
enduring in the practice of the past. The main way Catholics
have experienced this thrust is with regard to the Mass and
sacraments. Changes in the language of the Mass from
Latin to the vernacular, a more personalized approach to
the sacrament of Reconciliation, the streamlining of many
liturgical practices, modernization of church art and arch-
itecture—these are some commonly experienced effects of
aggiornamento.

Many have viewed *aggiornamento* principally as a way the
church is apologizing to the modern world for being old-
fashioned and out of date, and repenting of her sins by
abolishing outdated and medieval practices. There is some
truth to this statement. But the main purpose of *aggiornamento*
is not to adjust to what is *good* in the modern world, as
though the modern world has a better gospel than the
church, but to tailor the gospel more to its *weaknesses* and
problems in order that she might better minister salvation to
it. Thus, for example, John Paul II in *Laborem Exercens*, his
encyclical based on the council's approach to work in the
modern world, is not concerned mainly with the way modern man has freed much of the human race from difficulty
and drudgery in work, but with offering man a way out of
the enslavement to work he now finds himself in as a result
of the abuses of Marxism and rigid capitalism. His *Theology
of the Body* is designed, not to accept the sexual immorality
of today, but to give man a way to remain chaste and pure
in the modern environment.

Back to the Sources

The purpose of this thrust of the council is to move
Catholic consciousness away from textbook scholasticism
toward a style and means of expression which are based
mainly on the Bible and the Fathers of the church. Back to
the sources began to build momentum as a trend in the
church long before the council, and was the particular inter-
est of Pius XII's encyclical *Divino Afflante Spiritu*, written in

1943. One can see this thrust reflected in all areas of Catholic life today, and we most commonly experience its effects in liturgical life and the Catholic educational process.

A good example of how back to the sources works can be found in the first few sections of *Lumen Gentium*, the dogmatic constitution on the church. Rather than defining the church mainly in abstract, preconciliar terms, such as "the perfect hierarchical society," the document offers a vision of the church which relies heavily on scriptural images such as the flock, the temple and the pilgrim people.

The Pastoral Thrust

Pope John XXIII said many times that the council should be a pastoral council. By this he meant that the council should not focus on definitions, dogmas, rules, laws, etc., but should focus instead on how the church and the individual believer can grow in self-understanding with regard to what they believe. As John Paul II teaches, the purpose of the council was not mainly to say what we must believe, but "what it means to be a believer."* This pastoral thrust is reflected in the opening statement of the council, "Church, what do you say of yourself?"

A good example of the implementation of this thrust in the lives of the faithful is the change in the Friday-fast rules. Before the council, Catholics were forbidden to eat meat on Fridays. Most persons approached this policy in a legalistic way. Then, after the council, as we all know, the rule was changed. Many people thought the church was trying to make it easier to be Catholic or wanted to lift an old-fashioned rule. But the true pastoral intention of the church in making this change was that Catholics learn to fast and abstain by a *free* and *conscious* decision rather than by mindlessly obeying some rule, which is of little spiritual advantage anyway.

There are many, many examples of the implementation of the pastoral thrust of the council in today's church. The entire tone of the documents themselves is strongly pastoral.

Sources of Renewal, p. 17.

The spirit of this thrust is best summarized by a maxim from St. Augustine which was quoted often during the council: "In what is essential, unity; in what is doubtful, liberty, and in all things, charity."

An important thing to remember about the pastoral orientation of the council is that it was not meant to oppose the rules, dogmas or laws of the past, though it did change many rules and practices which were considered no longer helpful. Rather, the pastoral thrust was designed mainly to *complement* the dogmatic tone of the past and make it richer and more human.

Participation

Participation means drawing all members of the church—clergy, religious and laity—into greater active involvement at all levels of Catholic life. The turning around of the altar, use of lectors and extraordinary ministers of Communion, parish councils, adult-education programs and lay leadership of different movements in the church are examples of this thrust of the council. The charismatic prayer meeting, made possible by the council's recognition of the charismatic dimension of Christian life (which Cardinal Suenens worked hard to have inserted as part of the council documents), constitutes the most advanced implementation of the thrust of participation at the grass-roots level. At any meeting, participants are free to share, pray, speak the Lord's word, etc., in a way that formerly was reserved to those who were trained and appointed to do such things.

Greater participation in the decision-making process in the church, through the spread of the concept of collegiality, is probably the most profound change produced by this thrust. (Collegiality refers to the practice of giving the bishops a greater voice in pastoring the life of the whole church.) Whether it be on the level of bishops' synods and conferences, priests' senates, diocesan councils or parish councils, many more persons have input into the way the church discerns what it should do and how it should be.

Ecumenism

Ecumenism is different from the other major thrusts of the council in that it not only offers an enriched way of living as a Catholic, but it also has a clear future target in mind, the reunification of all Christians. Also, ecumenism often overlaps with other thrusts. Back to the sources, for example, is part of the ecumenical thrust in so far as it brings Catholics to a better appreciation of the Bible, which most Protestants already have. The thrust of dialogue, which we will consider below, is to be the foundation for all ecumenical conversations and projects. Participation brings Catholic ecclesiology closer to the more participatory approaches of most Protestant denominations.

Though many see ecumenism as being implemented mainly by engaging more in cooperative efforts with our separated brothers and sisters, the first priority with regard to this thrust, according to the mind of the council, is deeper conversion to Christ on the part of Catholics themselves and a more genuine living out of Catholic life. Unless this is done, all that is said about the need for reunification among Christians will be seen as a sham by those with whom we engage in ecumenical dialogue.

Dialogue

The final, and perhaps most significant thrust of the council is the change from a preconciliar, polemical posture to a posture of dialogue with regard to those outside the church. Dialogue involves relating to other "circles of dialogue" (Paul VI). These circles could be non-Catholic Christians, non-Christian believers, politicians, scientists, businessmen, atheists, etc. With a positive and open attitude we seek to engage them in fruitful and mutually enriching interchanges. One hoped-for fruit of dialogue is the enrichment of the individual's life through greater appreciation for what is good in other viewpoints. In addition, dialogue offers increased opportunities for witnessing to Christ's saving love in the context of a charitable exchange of views. Third, dialogue can increase the church's chances for peaceful coexistence with other circles of dialogue in society. The church understands that, in our time, mankind is becoming increasingly united through technology and mass communication, while at the same time is increasingly pluralistic in terms of the various philosophies and viewpoints which constantly struggle for survival and ascendancy. In this regard, dialogue calls for cooperative efforts with regard to practical points of agreement.

An example of the first type of fruit—that of enriching the individual's life—is found in the church's growth in appreciation for the Bible, which it learned from Protestant brothers and sisters. An example of the second type is the church's approach to the social problems of Latin America, through which she is trying to show to the masses of the poor and oppressed that she, as Christ's body on earth, truly loves the poor. An example of the third type is the church's way of dialoging with Communist countries, exemplified in Poland.

Another form of dialogue takes place within the church itself and not with other circles of dialogue. The purpose of this dialogue is to increase understanding, on all levels of Catholic life, of the deeper meaning of believing in Christ and being members of his church. Dialogue within the church, when conducted with honesty and with sound faith as a foundation, accomplishes this goal. In fact, such dialogue has always been going on in the church (though not at all levels) under the aspect of "faith seeking understanding."

Enrichment and Integration

These six thrusts, which in a simplified way represent all the enrichments of the council, do not in themselves constitute renewal. For authentic renewal to take place the *enrichments* of the council must be *integrated* back into what existed before the council and was already good. Thus, for example, the enrichment of collegiality is not authentically a renewal until it is implemented in the context of church teaching on papal authority, which is good and existed before the council. The new, more personalized approach to the sacrament of Reconciliation needs to be integrated back into a clear consciousness of the sinister and evil result of sin. Also, the Eucharist as community meal and celebration must be understood without losing sight of the preconciliar insight into the Eucharist as imparting divine life to each individual soul. And so on.

This then, in capsule form, is what was beginning to happen in the universal church during the preparation and progress of the council (1958-1965).

The 60s and 70s

The late 60s and 70s witnessed a kind of unravelling of the American Catholic life which had formerly been stable and strong. The pull of modern life on the Catholic consciousness was becoming increasingly strong as Catholics grew in affluence, as the media became increasingly secularized while their impact on life became more pervasive, and as ethnic Catholics gradually drifted out of their sheltered neighborhoods into the mainstream of American culture. Many of my friends and classmates began to lose their (perhaps naive) faith and morals. They began to sleep around and think nothing of getting drunk regularly. Some of them began to be habitual drug users. Meanwhile, some of their parents divorced each other. Many nuns left the convent. I remember that the three priests who were the embodiment of all that was best in my childhood Catholic life left the priesthood and got married.

In the midst of this unravelling, Vatican II was dropped on the Catholic consciousness "from above" (Rome). At first, many had great hopes that this new way of being Catholic would not only bring the church up to date, as it was first intended to do, but would also, just in the nick of time, reverse the unravelling of Catholic life that had begun to take place. It was the legalism, brittleness and authoritarianism of the preconciliar church that was at the source of this unravelling, many thought, and the new freedom and lofty vision of the council would provide the faithful with new vitality, propelling them forward into a new era of success in living the gospel. This was not to be the case. The unravelling continued and, for the most part, continues today.

Today

Many have left the church. Those who remain have set themselves up in several camps. I would like to label the camps, from "left to right" ("left" meaning their theological position with regard to Christianity being liberal and "right" meaning that it is conservative): *neo-Modernists, progressives, radicals, conservatives* and *integrists*. There is another camp, *casualties of dialogue*, which I will consider later.

Let us consider each camp and how it relates to the others.

Neo-Modernists

This camp basically takes the position that Vatican II reversed the church's negative stance against Modernist thought of the late 1800s and early 1900s. Modernists rejected the truth of doctrines and reinterpreted them as part of an evolving historical process in which "truth" is expressed according to one's place on the historical spectrum. Modernists also were skeptical about supernatural revelation of truth. They would have us think that, although the apostles really believed that Jesus physically rose from the dead, modern man need not believe this. With modern knowledge of ancient myth, science and history, we now know that the ancients were telling their story, their myth, but that our myth doesn't need to include the unlikely possibility, scientifically speaking, that Jesus really did physically rise from the dead.

These persons, by their intellectual stance, put themselves outside the church (though they protest that they are still in). The church has consistently condemned such an approach. There are, numerically speaking, few neo-Modernists, but they are very influential in the intellectual circles of the church. Some are writers and thinkers, and they teach in many seminaries and in Catholic (as well as secular) universities.

Progressives

Progressives take the position that Vatican II was a step in the right direction, but that we need more changes if the vision of the council is to prevail. They love the *enrichments* of the council, but are not very interested in *integration*. They tend to be very impatient with anyone to the right of them, and somewhat sympathetic of, though not approving, the neo-Modernists.

There are large numbers of progressives, both clergy and laity. Many younger priests in America are progressives, as are many younger, educated laymen and laywomen.

Radicals

The radicals, among them Paul VI and John Paul II, embrace fully the vision of the council, both in terms of its enrichments and in terms of the necessity for integration. They are usually the ones caught in the middle of debates between progressives and conservatives, and end up suffering the most for it. They are often described in the secular media as doctrinally conservative, but progressive with regard to pastoral and social issues. They seem to other camps to be strict and authoritarian at times, while dialogical and flexible at other times. From their own viewpoint, they are simply being consistent with the vision which the Holy Spirit offered the church in the council documents.

The radical camp is a small but growing group in the church. Many of the bishops appointed by the present pope are, not surprisingly, radicals. Cardinal Bernardin of Chicago is a good example. Many priests and laypersons, loyal to the pope, are gradually shifting from other camps to this camp as it becomes clear that the papal agenda for the church has a realistic chance of working.

Conservatives

This problem is marked by a strong regard for the preconciliar church and by a guardedness with regard to the enrichments of the council. Conservatives, while not openly attacking the enrichments, feel the need to warn continually about the dangers of implementing enrichments without integrating them into the good of the past. They are angry at the damage done to the church by the neo-Modernists, mistrustful of the progressives, and usually puzzled by the radicals, who seem to them to be oscillating between the conservative and progressive camps.

The majority of older priests and laity are conservative.

Integrists

Integrists are those in the church who believe that the vision of the council is erroneous. They believe that the council is the root cause of the unravelling of Catholic life. Some have even said that an evil spirit now influences the papacy.

These persons are few in number—although not so few as many progressives and neo-Modernists would like to think— but they are powerful in certain sectors of Catholic life.

The church has consistently rebuked those who take this position, just as it continually rebukes the neo-Modernists.

The Place of the Charismatic Renewal in our Historical Blueprint

The charismatic renewal, by which I mean the baptism in the Spirit and the normal set of experiences which follow it, is a manifestation of the *power of God for the implementation of the Second Vatican Council*. The council offers the vision for the new Pentecost, and the baptism in the Spirit provides charismatics with the power to implement the vision.

A look at the charismatic experience in terms of the six thrusts of the council, of enrichment and integration, and of the five camps of today's church shows clearly that the two phenomena—baptism in the Spirit and Vatican II—are meant to complement each other.

With regard to *aggiornamento* (remembering that its main purpose is to minister to modern problems) the Holy Spirit uses the renewal to strike at perhaps the key problem of modern man, which is his despiritualization, his loss of soul, his becoming one-dimensional and materialistic, his rejection of God in the name of science, etc. However one phrases the problem, it is clear that man's drift away from spiritual realities is at the source of his present malaise. The baptism in the Spirit, viewed from the standpoint of this problem, brings about an acute respiritualization of consciousness. One reason why the experience is often so unwieldy and seemingly out-of-control is that it usually involves a violent break with one's prior negative attitude toward the spiritual. I have never found it surprising that persons, upon being filled with the Spirit, sometimes begin to see demons everywhere, or look for spiritual clues with regard to every decision they make, or lose emotional control, and so on. They were deeply unspiritual in their habitual perspective before being filled with the Spirit, and have realized how profoundly mistaken their old view of life was. It is only natural that, for a time at least, they will err in the other direction.

There are other examples of the Holy Spirit implementing his call to *aggiornamento* in the charismatic renewal, but this is the most evident and most important one, and serves, I believe, to illustrate that conciliar *aggiornamento* is implemented in the renewal.

With regard to going back to the sources, the charismatic renewal is clearly the most advanced instance of its grassroots implementation. Those of us who are active in the renewal know from daily experience that the Spirit, when he fills us and leads us on, is constantly enriching our understanding of and appreciation for his word in scripture.

The charismatic renewal is, as much as anything else, a Bible movement. It calls us back to the Bible; it seeks to implement biblical ideals and usually causes us to view our lives in terms of a biblical consciousness.

With regard to the patristic aspect of back to the sources, the renewal needs to do more. But its spiritual approach to the scriptures (as opposed to the historical-critical and some other modern approaches), its reverence for them, and its searching them for answers are already quite similar to the patristic way of approaching the bible. How often have those of us who know something about patristic thought, when hearing a good charismatic teaching on scripture, commented, "That sounds like something right out of the Fathers."

An attitude which is strongly *pastoral*, as opposed to one based on following rules without knowing what they mean, usually is present in charismatic life. People do not join prayer groups because they feel obligated. They do so freely. Each step they take by way of becoming more involved is a free one which is made with a heart understanding of what is being done rather than a concern that they will be punished or will have sinned if they don't do what is right.

Much of charismatic life centers around solving personal pastoral problems that arise in the lives of members. Although added difficulties often result when these problems are not successfully addressed, the fact that persons in the renewal have the courage and generosity to face the more complex, pastorally oriented way of being Christian called for by the council is a sign of the power of the Spirit at work in us.

The thrust of participation is also implemented in a profound way in the renewal. As has already been pointed out, the weekly charismatic prayer meeting is about as participatory a Christian gathering as one could possibly experience. Anyone can share. The lowliest lay person can speak the word of the Lord to the holiest religious or priest. All sing together. All can pray aloud together, each in his own words. Wisdom and teaching come when the Lord sends such impulses. None who views himself as a spectator at such meetings will do so for long if he or she is open to the Lord, because the Lord will probably say or do something for this individual before the meeting ends.

The charismatic renewal, in so far as it is a way for us to discover our particular function in Christ's body, resolves a question which can be a major obstacle in today's church to authentic participation, that is, how does one participate? We cannot all be leaders or priests or healers. Through the renewal, the Spirit can clarify for the individual the specific way in which he or she is called to participate more actively in building the body of Christ.

With regard to ecumenism, again, the evidence is clear. There is no other movement in the church where grass-roots ecumenism is taking place with the earnestness and depth that one sees in the renewal. The renewal was ecumenical from the start. Were it not for our brothers and sisters in the Pentecostal denominations, there would probably be no charismatic renewal. Their assistance and input were invaluable. Through the ongoing ecumenical dialogue that has taken place since then—and which continues today—both Catholics and non-Catholics have experienced in a deep way the enrichment of life which conciliar teaching on ecumenical dialogue leads us to expect.

Regarding the underlying methodology of enrichment and integration, responsible leadership in the renewal has from the start sought ways to integrate the enrichments of the renewal into the mainstream of the church. Renewed appreciation of the sacraments, deeper understanding of Catholic spirituality, a stronger sense of following apostolic authority in the papacy, the hierarchy and on the level of the parish— these are some examples of the many integrations of charismatic enrichment that are common in our experience.

With regard to the five camps in the church, the fullness of the Spirit also has a positive impact. For the church to be renewed, these camps must be reunited around the conciliar vision. The charismatic experience is used by the Lord to move those in the various camps closer to the council's vision. Radicals see that their problem is one of lack of power and gladly embrace the Spirit as the one who gives them the vitality to go on. Progressives, upon being filled with the Spirit, gain a new appreciation for the tradition of the church and, in particular, for its authority. They also receive a grace of charity for those conservatives with whom they were formerly so impatient. Conservatives, on the other hand, overcome their overly cautious and defensive position, and become willing to embrace the conciliar vision. Those camps outside the church, to the left and right, are often brought to repentance and freed from their pride, anger, lust and bitterness, which are usually at the root of their erroneous positions.

In the above discussion, I have avoided mentioning the difficulties encountered in the renewal with regard to its enrichments when they are not integrated well. Admittedly, *aggiornamento* too often produces parting with "dead traditions" which are actually not dead at all, but authentic and life-giving. Back to the Bible can lead to a "scripture only" consciousness with little respect for sacred tradition. For "pastoral" reasons, many slip away from their adherence to true doctrines. Participation can result in contempt for valid authority as though it keeps one from active participation. Ecumenism can lead some to lack of appreciation for loyalty to the visible church. Many charismatics "dialogue" themselves out of the church through naively embracing evangelical revivalism.

I have chosen to analyze manifestations of the renewal which stay clear of the above-mentioned abuses. I have done this to demonstrate how the charismatic experience, when it unfolds *according to the Lord's plan*, implements the vision of Vatican II with power.

I do not mean to imply that there are no other examples of the implementation of the council. Certainly this is not the case. I do mean to say that those of us who have experienced the baptism in the Spirit in the right way have been implementing the Vatican Council and have played a part in unifying members of the different camps, whether we know it or not. I mean also to say to those who are not charismatic that the baptism in the Spirit and the set of experiences which accompanies it (if a person stays on course) allow one to implement the vision of the council with spiritual power which a person would not possess otherwise.

The Future

The future of the church is the implementation of the vision of the council. For this to take place, the various camps in the church must come to a greater unity. The integrists and the neo-Modernists, however well-intentioned they may have been, must do some serious soul-searching. They are seriously in error and are currently doing great damage to the church. Progressives must integrate; conservatives must enrich. All camps must unite around the papal vision—which is the radical vision—forgetting what is past and "purifying their hearts," as Cardinal Bernardin taught his priests during his installation in Chicago in August of 1982. All must sincerely seek authentic renewal in the Holy Spirit, whether they call it baptism in the Spirit or something else. The conciliar vision is a very difficult one to implement. We did not have the power to do it when it was first proclaimed. We need that power, which is the power of God himself. The charismatic renewal may well be an experiment of the Lord which is meant to serve as a model for the whole church in the future. What happens when God the Holy Spirit comes to our modern world? What will it look like? How should we react? Twenty years ago, we had no answers other than some theories. Now we know, through the renewal, some of what might take place.

Casualties of Dialogue

I would like to end this chapter by discussing a camp in the church that is very large, but which is seldom understood or ministered to effectively. It is made up of those who are "casualties of dialogue." These are persons who, through some kind of contact with the council's teaching on dialogue, were led into a way of thinking that resulted in their leaving the church, or least abandoning belief in some of its teachings. There are many types of persons who are casualties of dialogue. I know Catholic scientists who, in dialogue with non-Christian scientists on the meaning of the theory of evolution, have ended up believing that original sin and the fall of man are not evil in the sense that the church has always taught. They think that such evils are necessary parts of God's plan for evolutionary progress and are actually good in the long run. (How else could we make progress?) This leads them into the heresy that there is no hell, and into the belief that God wanted evil to come into the world. Both positions put them outside the faith.

I know many theologians and priests who, in dialogue with liberal Protestant thinkers, have come to believe that the historicity of many events in Christ's life, such as the resurrection, are questionable and not even very important. This also constitutes a break with Christian truth as it has been revealed by God.

I know of some religious leaders who, in dialoguing with powerful businessmen and politicians, end up compromising their Christian moral principles on issues such as abortion and sexual morality, and deceive those who look to them for guidance into thinking such compromises are permissible in light of pastoral, political and economic realities.

I know of many ill-intentioned persons who deliberately try to produce casualties of dialogue in an attempt to weaken the church. They are often in some teaching position in the Catholic educational system. The confusion they produce is not due to their ignorance or inability to handle dialogue, as is often the case with some other casualties of dialogue. They really want their listeners to change their beliefs. They want to spread confusion about the faith because they are enemies of Christianity as it is taught and lived in the Catholic Church.

However, the overwhelming majority of casualties of dialogue are persons who have lost their faith while young, as a result of exposure to dialogue in the Catholic educational process. Most of us know at least a few of these persons. They may be our children. We may have even been in this group at some time in our lives. I would like to discuss how such persons become casualties of dialogue and make some suggestions as to how they can be brought back to the Lord.

As I already mentioned, while in high school in the mid-60s I began to notice that many of my friends at school were losing their faith. I became distressed at this and asked a priest at the school (which was a Catholic school) what could be done about the situation. He told me not to worry. This was a phase my friends were going through, he explained; after they had experienced their crisis of faith, they would return to God. But, as time passed and we all moved into adult life, very few of them recovered their faith. Today, 18 years later, only two of a dozen high school friends who had crises of faith call themselves Christian in the religious sense.

After high school, my friends and I would get together from time to time, and I would try to persuade them to return to the Lord. Although my efforts were unsuccessful, these get-togethers were occasions for searching reflection on my part as to the real causes of my friends' loss of faith. I gradually came to the conclusion that, though many factors had to be taken into account (e.g., drug use, confusion about modern life, deliberate rejection of God), the biggest factor in their abandonment of faith was the failure of the Catholic educational system to communicate Christian truth to them adequately.

I taught high-school religion in the mid-70s and saw the same kind of unravelling of faith taking place in the lives of my students. I tried to reverse the process but was unsuccessful. I now found myself part of the system that was allowing the unravelling to take place. This served to increase my distress about the problem and caused me to search more diligently for some kind of solution.

A story told me recently by a couple whose son lost his faith in high school in the 60s gave me more insight into the problem. Their son's high school was one of several in the diocese which had experimented with Vatican II's dialogical approach to being Catholic. On the level of the educational process, dialogue calls on Catholics to cultivate a solid intellectual understanding of Catholic truth. This would give the learner mature and authentic ground to stand on as he or she enters into dialogue with other circles of dialogue.

In religion class, such an approach would entail looking into what is of value in other religions, in modern psychology, science, philosophy, etc., while looking at one's own faith less blindly, with a greater emphasis on "what it means to be a believer," not just on what one believes.

In the process of the experiment, many students had become casualties of the dialogical approach. They did not believe in Christ anymore. At a diocesan meeting of parents, teachers and administrators attended by the mother, this new way of teaching religion was proclaimed a success in spite of the casualties. The mother, whose son was a casualty of dialogue, asked the monsignor who was leading the meeting, "What about the kids who can't handle this new, questioning approach and lose their faith?" The monsignor's response was, "Well, we expect to lose a few." Needless to say, the woman was furious at having her son dismissed as an inevitable statistical casualty. She felt abandoned by the people she had entrusted with the preservation of her son's faith. Not only had they not preserved it; she believed they had actually helped destroy it. As the years passed and it became clear that the monsignor's "few" had become the majority of students, promoters of the new way of doing things became significantly less enthusiastic about what they had done.

The cause of this problem is not dialogue itself but, rather, the mishandling of conciliar teaching on dialogue by many Catholic educators. The teaching on dialogue, which is designed to assist the church in surviving in and witnessing to the modern world, is crucial to being Christian today, but it is not an easy teaching to implement. It calls for a much more sophisticated way of relating to persons, groups and ideas than the preconciliar, polemical approach. Successful dialogue requires a good deal of training and preparation. According to church teaching on the subject one must be spiritually mature, prudent, honest, patient, in harmony with church authority, free of jargon and manipulation, etc.

What are some of the issues facing a high-school religion teacher who wants to prepare young Christians for dialogue in contemporary society—a society which questions everything about religion? Say, for example, he teaches them something that they will inevitably hear from another source— that, from the standpoint of historical honesty, one cannot know for sure that the biblical story of Noah and the ark is more than a myth which is meant to teach a lesson. He must be careful that, while learning such a thing, his students' faith in the resurrection (another biblical story) as a real, historical event is safeguarded. He also needs to be sure that parents, who are the primary religious educators of their children, understand what he is doing, so that they do not become involved in disputes at home over differing approaches to such an issue. Throughout it all, he needs to remember James's warning that those who teach will be judged more strictly by the Lord (Jas. 3:1).

Unfortunately, teachers too often neglect taking the kind of care and precaution that must accompany the dialogical approach. They feel fine about shocking their students into a crisis of faith, which in most cases results in a loss of faith. These students lose their spiritual moorings almost without thinking, and look back, wondering what happened and feeling that they have made a mistake. But they quickly overcome their anxieties with the pat answers of secularism: "I have to decide what I think." "If there is a God, he isn't like they say he is." "At least I'm honest." Parents, exasperated with teachers and with their children, either entrench themselves in the polemics of the past and alienate themselves from their children, or, for the sake of family peace, embrace the carelessly implemented type of dialogue practiced by the teachers and become casualties of dialogue themselves.

What must be done? We cannot continue on the present course. Contrary to the assurances that clergy and religious still give worried parents, most casualties are not returning. They may never return. What then? Should we reject dialogue as a colossal pastoral error and return to the polemics of the past? Only if we think the modern world is suddenly going to disappear. No, we cannot take this road, either.

We must do three things. First, we must seek the power of God. The Lord, by the special grace of the fullness of his Spirit, has already brought thousands of casualties of dialogue back to himself and to love for his church. In the charismatic renewal, many participants speak of how their doubts, crises, skepticism and confusion about truth were resolved as they were filled with the Spirit. Perhaps more than any other single phenomenon, the release of the Spirit has won casualties back to the Lord.

Second, we must bring to a halt the ill-conceived and poorly implemented style of dialogue that is practiced in the church today. All Catholics, especially those who have any teaching responsibility, should carefully study the wisdom of the council fathers before they begin to implement this important teaching of Vatican II. The reading of the conciliar documents is a good starting point, along with Paul VI's encyclical, *Ecclesiam Suam*, in which he teaches, "Before we can convert the world—nay, in order to convert it—we must first meet the world and talk to it."

Finally, we must recognize that the witness of Christian love is the key way to bring casualties of dialogue back to the Lord. In my conversation with the couple who were concerned over their son's loss of faith, we eventually came to the point where we asked, what can one do now? The father answered that, in his experience, arguing the issues was useless, and the only thing they could do now (other than pray for their son) was to give witness to Christ by greater charity toward him. His hope was that, as their son saw the fruit of their lives, he would realize that they, as Christians, had the true answer to the meaning of life.

The father's final observation offers a clue to the Lord's deeper purpose in calling his church into a dialogical posture and to the conciliar vision on the whole. It may be his way of pastoring us to a greater commitment to love one another. "Dialogue is the way to enrich faith not only because it increases the maturity of conviction but also, and above all, because thanks to it faith becomes particularly strong, vivified as it is by love."* Through it, a milieu is created in which formalistic, conventional ways of relating are insufficient, and in which our contribution as members of the church is much more decisive than it was in the days when we could depend on the priests, religious and saints to keep the faith going. If we—the ordinary rank-and-file laypersons—do not make the effort, the faith of our children, friends and even our whole society may be lost. Let us get fixed in our minds the truth that we have a real burden and responsibility for the future of the church, and let us respond in kind, accepting the fullness of the Spirit and implementing the vision of Vatican II.

Sources of Renewal, p. 34.

CHAPTER 2:

Catholic Spirituality

When viewed as a movement which enriches one's spiritual life, the charismatic renewal can rightly be labelled the most significant and widespread enrichment of spirituality among Catholics since the beginning of the conciliar era. Perhaps as many as 20,000,000 Catholics have experienced, to some degree, the life-changing spiritual effects of the baptism in the Spirit. However, remembering John Paul II's teaching that authentic conciliar renewal must not only *enrich* one's Catholic faith but must also *integrate* it into what was already good before the council, we must ask, does the charismatic experience integrate a person's spiritual life into the traditional Catholic framework?

The answer is yes, although such integration is not always done consciously. Traditional Catholic teaching on the spiritual life is structured around the seven gifts of the Spirit

For a more complete treatment of the material covered in this chapter, see my book *Mighty in Spirit* (Charismatic Renewal Services, 1982). This chapter summarizes the material from that book and places it in the larger context of Catholic thought covered in this book.

listed in Isaiah 11* and the seven virtues which lead to and
flow from these gifts. Life in the Spirit includes the experience of these seven Isaiah gifts and leads a person to seek
growth in the virtues which are connected with them. This
happens in spite of the fact that charismatics do not normally view their lives in terms of the traditional framework.

In this chapter, we will discuss how the enriching experience of life in the Spirit can be viewed according to the
traditional perspective. In the course of our discussion, advice will be offered on how charismatics can integrate their
spirituality more into the Catholic framework by becoming
more aware of their "Isaiah-giftedness" and also through
implementing the wisdom of the church on how to cultivate
these gifts.

In our presentation, we follow a pattern which is somewhat different from the traditional pattern of presenting the
seven gifts. Traditional discussions of the seven gifts are
structured in the following way: The seven gifts of the Holy
Spirit—wisdom, understanding, knowledge, counsel, piety,
might and fear of the Lord—are seen as the perfections of
the seven virtues—faith, hope, love, prudence, justice
fortitude and temperance. The traditional framework, which
was taught by the fathers of the church, especially by Pope
St. Gregory the Great in the *Moralia,* and further developed
by St. Thomas Aquinas, connects each gift with a virtue and
shows how, as a person grows in the practice of each virtue,
he comes closer to the point where he will begin to be open
to the reception of the gift. There is a sense of ascending
actively by means of practicing the virtues to the point
where one becomes open to the reception of gifts, through
which the Spirit acts in us rather than us doing most of the
acting. Reflecting this notion, John of St. Thomas wrote,
"By the virtues we walk; by the gifts we fly."

In charismatic life, almost the reverse process occurs. It
seems that the giftedness by which we "fly" comes at the
beginning of our life in the Spirit, and, taking the traditional
framework as the norm, the Lord wants us to work backward,
so to speak, to fill in the gaps in virtue in our spiritual lives.

*Isaiah 11: 1-4, Septuagint and Vulgate

We start with an initial manifestation of the gifts and, in order to preserve that giftedness and grow in it, we need to practice greater virtue.

Hence, as we treat each of the seven gifts, we will describe what the gift looks like in charismatic life and then show how it can be preserved and strengthened by founding it more firmly on the virtue connected with it in the traditional framework. Thus, fear of the Lord is cultivated by growing in hope and temperance, might by fortitude, piety by justice, and so on.

Fear of the Lord

Fear of the Lord is a heartfelt attitude of reverence and awe toward the Lord which causes us to honor and obey him. When we are filled with the Spirit, we normally begin to experience this gift to some degree. It comes to us in the form of a new wonder at the goodness and greatness of the Lord. We become aware of how he is infinitely good and powerful, how he created us out of his goodness, how he keeps us in existence, forgives us, has mercy on us, cares for us, etc. We experience a newfound reverence for him, especially when we pray. The prayers of the Mass, such as the "Glory to God" and the "Holy, Holy," or psalms such as the Hallel Psalms (112 to 117) take on a deeper meaning for us.

Often this gift is most evident to us when we are at Mass and are receiving Communion. One senses at charismatic liturgies a special feeling in the hearts of participants, a sense of wonder at the mystery of the Body and Blood of Christ, a sense not always present at noncharismatic liturgies.

Usually, however, we fail to make full use of this gift of the Spirit because we associate it with the problem of being afraid of God, a difficulty which is normally overcome through the release of the Spirit. Before experiencing the baptism in the Spirit, many tend to relate to the Lord mainly as a distant, fearsome judge, but afterward they come to know him as a close, intimate, personal friend. Fear is seen as a negative way of relating to him, and the fear of the Lord is mistakenly associated with it, so it is not embraced as the wonderful gift that it actually is.

We can overcome this difficulty by understanding that the gift of fear of the Lord involves emotions of awe and wonder—as opposed to the emotion of fear—and by clarifying for ourselves the proper place of fear in spiritual growth.

Tradition teaches that there are four types of fear. The first type is worldly or mundane fear. This kind of fear is evil, since it is a fear of the opinions of men, the loss of material comfort, or the loss of one's earthly life. The second kind of fear is called "servile" fear, which causes us to do good out of fear of punishment. It is good to have servile fear, at least at the start of one's life in Christ. Jesus himself recommends it several times in the Gospels. For example, he tells us, "If your hand or your foot causes you to sin, cut it off . . . , better to enter life maimed or lame than with two hands or feet to be thrown into the eternal fire" (Mt. 18:8). The third type of fear, which is also good, is chaste fear, or fear of being separated from one's beloved. This fear exists in a person who practices the fear of the Lord, since even those who are mature in Christ do good so that they will not be separated from the Lord, their beloved. The fourth kind of fear is called initial fear. This fear, which we experience when we first come to know the Lord, (hence the name, "initial") is a mixture of the second and third types. We want to avoid punishment but, in addition, having experienced the love of the Lord, we do not want to be separated from him again, and so we do his will.

As we grow in our dedication to the Lord, we can use fear of punishment to motivate ourselves to avoid sin. But, as we come to know him more and more, this fear will gradually die out in us and only the fear of possibly being separated from him will remain. For those who attain a certain perfection in loving the Lord, even his fear is no longer present. At this point, as the scripture says, "Perfect love casts out fear" (1 Jn. 4:18).

The practice of the virtues of hope and temperance, which tradition connects with fear of the Lord, can also help us grow in this gift. Fear of the Lord and hope "cling to one another," as St. Thomas says,* because the gift of fear impels us to stay in a state of reverence toward the Lord so that we will honor and obey him and thus sustain the virtue of hope for salvation. Fear of the Lord, which involves the "hatred of evil" (Pr. 8:13) leads us to shun especially the aspects of evil that seduce our reason, which is the concern of the virtue of temperance.

Hope is the stretching of a person's will toward the attainment of a difficult but reachable goal. For the Christian, hope has two difficult but attainable goals: eternal happiness with the Lord in heaven and the coming of his kingdom on earth. The release of the Spirit greatly increases our capacity for hope with regard to both these goals. Our confidence that the Lord intends for us to be with him in heaven is strengthened as we come to know him intimately as a merciful and compassionate Lord. In an era when many are despairing of the church's ability to bring about the Lord's rule on earth, life in the Spirit offers participants new and fresh hope for how this can be brought about.

As we grow in Spirit-filled hope, we need to avoid the tendency to aim too high in terms of our hopes for earthly progress in bringing about the Lord's kingdom. True hope must be grounded in realistic possibilities. Many charismatics, unwilling to face the difficulties involved in striving toward the goals which true hope aims at, indulge themselves in wishful thinking and grandiose visions which are never fulfilled. Such an approach can actually weaken a person's hope and eventually lead to discouragement, despair and loss of vision.

Temperance (moderation, self-control) is the virtue by which we overcome sins that allure us by keeping us from obeying our reason. As we become more conscious of the presence of the Lord in our lives through fear of the Lord, we develop an aversion to these sins, which mainly involve the vices of lust, gluttony, anger and pride. We experience such sins as disturbing the peace and joy which the Spirit has given us, and so we work harder than we might have to

*ST,II,II,q.19,a9.

uproot them from our lives. Virtues such as humility, modesty, self-discipline, continence with regard to food, and meekness become important habits to cultivate.

In charismatic life, we need to guard against using the freedom we experience in the Spirit as an excuse for not growing in the self-control and discipline that temperance calls for. Too often, when we fail to live temperately because of the difficulty involved in bringing our fleshly desires under control, we dismiss our failures with thoughts such as, The Lord understands, or, He loves me and will forgive me. Though these statements are true, they should cause us to work even harder to overcome what stands between us and him, rather than leaving us in a situation of habitually sinning.

As we continue to practice fear of the Lord and the virtues of hope and temperance that are connected with it, we can look forward to greater power and freedom in the Spirit. "The angel of the Lord encamps around those who fear him" (Ps. 34:7). "The fear of the Lord leads to life" (Pr. 19:23). "The fear of the Lord is glory and splendor" (Sir. 1:9). "The fear of the Lord is a fountain of life" (Pr. 14:27). "The fear of the Lord prolongs life" (Pr. 10:21). "In the fear of the Lord one has strong confidence" (Pr. 14:26). All these things and more are promised to those who practice the fear of the Lord.

Might

Might (strength, courage, fortitude) is the gift of the Spirit which enables us to face with strength and confidence the trials and dangers we encounter in the Christian life. When we are filled with the Spirit, might usually manifests itself as a newfound confidence about oneself. The problems which a person encounters in daily life that formerly seemed so difficult to live with are easier to handle. Often, a person experiences a newfound ability to witness to others about the gospel.

Might is crucial to living in the Spirit, particularly when following the Lord becomes difficult. Though we experience it immediately when we accept the fullness of the Spirit, the need for it does not always become evident until the initial first grace of the release of the Spirit begins to fade and the Lord returns us to a spiritual state in which living the Christian life becomes more difficult. Unfortunately, rather than claiming and using the gift of might at this point, we tend to weaken and grow discouraged.

As a first step in cultivating the gift of might, we need to value it rightly and learn to draw on it when the Lord sends us trials such as the ones we face when he withdraws some of the initial consolations of the baptism in the Spirit. We must recognize that might and the patient endurance which it leads to are just as much fruit of the Spirit as love, joy and peace, though the latter bring with them more pleasant feelings.

We can also cultivate might through the practice of the virtue of fortitude. Fortitude is the virtue by which we grow in our ability to do what might supernaturally empowers us to do, i.e., face the difficulties, trials and dangers of life with strength and confidence in the Lord. Scripture and tradition offer advice on how to grow in fortitude along the lines of three themes: patience, perseverance and great-heartedness (magnanimity).

Patience, which in Greek means "great-temperedness," is traditionally defined as the bearing of trials in a joyful and peaceful spirit. Rejoicing in the midst of suffering is an oft-repeated theme in the New Testament: e.g., "We rejoice in our suffering" (Rom. 5:3). "Count it all joy, my brethren, when you meet various trials" (Jas. 1:2). The sufferings we endure as Christians are used by the Lord to train and form us, and the cultivation of patience—joyful and peaceful forbearance—in the midst of these sufferings enables the Lord to work more quickly to bring us to maturity.

Scripture also calls on us to persevere in our lives in Christ. "He who endures to the end will be saved" (Mt. 10:22). This seems simple enough advice to follow, but it bears consideration. We know that, to some degree, most of us fail from time to time to persevere on the path the Lord is leading us. When we do fail, we are usually in the habit of making various and often complicated excuses.

But usually the problem is quite simple—we don't "hang in there," as Fr. John Bertolucci has so often exhorted charismatics to do. We quit. As part of growing in perseverance we need to take a simple enough approach to it so that we do not talk ourselves out of persevering by means of overanalysis or rationalization.

The practice of great-heartedness or heroism, which involves the accomplishing of great and difficult deeds for the Lord, is sorely lacking in the pampered, modern consciousness out of which most charismatics come. This virtue is spoken of often in the New Testament, usually along the lines of imitating those great saints who went before us. Hebrews 11, for example, tells of the great deeds of our forefathers in faith. Then, at the end of the section, it says, "Therefore, since we are surrounded by so great a cloud of witnesses, let us lay aside every weight that clings so closely, and run the race with perseverance" (Heb. 11:12). A key way to grow in Christian heroism is to learn about the heroes of faith and let our hearts be stirred up to imitate them in their great deeds. We may even be acquainted personally with someone who lives in such a way as to stir us up to overcome our mediocrity and weakness.

The gift of might, when it comes to maturity in us, will give us a relentless vigor in the Spirit. Along with St. Paul, we will cease "looking at what is past, but press onward toward the upward call in Christ Jesus" (Phil. 3:14). As we grow in might, we will become heroic in our Christian lives. Others will look to us for inspiration, just as we have looked to the heroes who came before us. We will experience deep joy and peace as we endure the sufferings of our lives. Filled with the Spirit of Christ, we will see suffering the way he saw it. "For the joy that was set before him, he endured death on the cross" (Heb. 12:2).

Piety

The gift of piety, called in scripture the "spirit of adoption" (Rom. 8:15), is that manifestation of the Spirit which produces in us a loving and worshipful consciousness of God as our Father. It is a common part of the charismatic experience, not only when we are first filled with the Spirit, but also in an ongoing way. This is evidenced by the fact that, in most prayer groups, the loving fatherly care of God is a regular prophetic theme.

Piety affects us at a deep level of our souls. As we are taught by the Spirit to cry out, "*Abba*, Father" (literally "papa" or "daddy"), we sense an enormous breakthrough in our relationship with the Father. So many feelings of distance, guilt and fear which may have marked our prior attitude toward him are cleansed from our hearts as we are given a profound sense of filial closeness to him. Images of a wrathful judge or unconcerned Creator give way to the true image of our Father as merciful, gracious, slow to anger, abounding in steadfast love, faithful and forgiving (though also firm and just).

As we strive to grow in the gift of piety, many of us may be hindered in our efforts by having a wrong notion of what it means to be a father. This usually is the result of either our past experience of deficient fatherhood in our personal lives or a warped notion of what true fatherhood means which we learned from the media and the educational system. We can correct this problem by looking to scripture and adopting its understanding of what a father is. The model of the father of the prodigal son (Lk. 14), of the father who loved his wayward children so much that he sent his only son to save them (Jn. 3:16), and other scriptural models can show us the meaning of the concept of fatherhood as the Lord would have us understand it. The example of Jesus, the perfect son, who did nothing on his own but only what his Father told him (Jn. 7:16), who counted on him for protection (Mt. 26:52), etc., gives us a pattern for how we as good children can practice true filial piety toward our Father.

The practice of the virtue of justice is the foundation on which the gift of piety is built. In the Christian life, justice means more than simple obedience to laws and rules (not lying, cheating, stealing, etc.). It involves striving, in all situations, to treat every person as having dignity and value as a child of our heavenly Father.

Tradition offers sound teaching along a number of lines

about how to implement the virtue of justice. With regard to material things, we must not only refuse to lie, cheat, steal, etc., but should be as free as possible from unnecessary debts. We should also take care of the property of others as though it were our own—or even more so, as if it were our heavenly Father's.

The most important possession a person has is his reputation. We must preserve the good name of others in all our relationships.

Faithfulness to religious obligations, such as tithing, keeping the Lord's day, etc., being good family members, good citizens and cooperating in a general way with those who are in authority in our lives—all these are important aspects of the virtue of justice. When we cooperate with those who are in rightful authority, we are indirectly obeying the Lord, since "there is no authority except from the Lord" (Rom. 13:1).

There are some key character traits which will further enrich our experience of piety. One is gratitude, which is the habit of freely responding to gifts, which are given freely, by freely giving gifts in return. First, of course, we need to cultivate gratitude toward God himself, who freely gave his only Son for our sakes. We can do this by freely giving our whole lives to him, and not just what we feel we owe him as a debt. We can also cultivate gratitude toward others who freely give of themselves for our sake. Parents, for example, who freely bring us into the world and care for us, deserve our gratitude, which we can show by honoring them, caring for them, etc.

Another trait we can cultivate is truthfulness. The bending of the story, the little white lie, and other such habits, though they may do no great damage, will weaken us in our pursuit of a just and pious heart before the Lord.

Friendliness or affability is a common trait in charismatic circles but is not often associated with the virtue of justice. In fact, however, not only should we be friendly to others out of the abundance of our joy in the Lord, but we should do it with a sense of obligation. All persons are created by the Lord with great dignity, and one small but important way to acknowledge that dignity is through the practice of friendliness and affection.

As the Lord fills us more and more with his Spirit of piety, we can look forward to many blessings. We will begin to love our Father with a love that comes from deep within our hearts. We will have great confidence in him and in his guiding and protecting hand over us. As we grow in our consciousness of God as our Father, we will experience a deeper sense of brotherhood/sisterhood with other Christians, and with all persons, since they are God's children.

Counsel

Counsel is the gift that empowers us to make decisions in the Spirit in practical life situations. When we are filled with the Spirit, counsel manifests itself as a new instinct that we suddenly seem to have acquired for making good decisions. We just seem to know the right thing to do and get an immediate clear sense of what his will is. Sometimes he seems to speak a direct word to us (charismatics often call this "personal prophecy"); other times we experience a sense of peace about a certain direction; other times we open to a passage in scripture which shows us the way to go. We seem in some situations to be able to make good choices about things when there was no way we could come to a good decision by reasoning alone, because the issue under consideration was too complex. It is at these times that we most clearly experience the presence of the gift of counsel.

However, the charismatic experience of counsel often results in confusion and disillusionment if it is not rightly understood. This can happen, for example, when we get a word from the Lord about some issue, while someone else gets a conflicting word which he claims is also from the Lord. The resulting dispute over what the Lord is really saying leads to more trouble than there would have been if there had been no words from the Lord at all.

To cite another example, we may experience a great deal of success in following counsel from the Lord and then, for a reason we do not understand, we begin to make what

turn out to be wrong choices, even though we feel we are
following the same kinds of leadings from the Lord. Usually
we follow these inspirations for a while, thinking that the
Lord is testing us or leading us through some kind of
difficult time. In the end, we become skeptical about the
Lord ever having given us any counsels.

Another type of difficulty often surfaces as we try to live
by the Lord's counsels. We begin to develop the view that
all decisions must be made by means of these direct counsels.
We look for spiritual discernment when common sense has
already provided the right answer. We tend to become
suspicious of reasonable approaches to decision-making,
thinking that they are human or even carnal ways of
operating, and that the Lord works differently. Even if the
fruit of this approach is not good, we sometimes cling to it,
thinking that, if we abandon it, we will be unfaithful to the
Lord because he is working in some mysterious way that we
do not yet understand. The final result is that we adopt a
spirituality which borders on illuminism, an abuse into which
many persons in religious movements have fallen over the
centuries.

We need to protect the manifestation of the gift of counsel
in our charismatic lives by not falling prey to discouragement or skepticism if the gift seems to fail us at times, while,
on the other hand, guarding against illuminism through
the practice of the virtue of prudence.

We can avoid becoming discouraged at the apparent failure of what we feel are the Lord's counsels if we simply
understand that counsel is a gift that allows for levels of
maturity. The Spirit abides in us more richly as we follow
him over the course of time, and the gift of counsel grows
apace. Thus, we need not feel tied down to what we feel are
his present counsels (or lack of counsels) in the same way
that we might feel bound by prophecy. We have to allow for
mistakes on our part, especially when we are new in the
Holy Spirit. As we grow, counsels will gradually become
more dependable and consistent in our lives.

Prudence, through which we can counter the charismatic
tendency toward illuminism, is the applying of sound reason to practical action. There are several rules of thumb to

follow in growing in this virtue. First, we must be sure to learn from past experiences, especially our mistakes. Second, we should be open to the sound advice of those who are more mature in Christ. They can save us the trouble of having to learn from our mistakes by warning us about them before we make them. Third, we must not be afraid of using common sense when it is called for. Here we need to find the right balance between being "super-spiritual" and slipping into a worldly approach to choices. Fourth, we must develop the habit of foresight, planning for the future as much as we can in the Lord. This habit must be cultivated while maintaining a readiness to respond to any change in plans the Lord may lead us to.

A final rule of thumb for the fostering of prudence in our lives is being cautious in the right way. We would not want to become so cautious as to quench the Spirit, but, at the same time, we should habitually take into account, to a reasonable degree, all the circumstances surrounding our choices as we move forward. Most of all, we need to take our own weakness and sinfulness into account.

Counsel gives the Spirit-filled person a sure guide for life. It helps overcome scruples, which can be a debilitating problem for serious Christians. Counsel also opens us up to the wise counsels of others in the body of Christ. No one person in the body is meant to have all the answers, and counsel enables us to listen more intently to what the Lord is saying to us about our decisions through others. Counsel is essential to the effective leadership of the church. Many complex problems need to be dealt with to move the body of Christ forward at every level, whether it be in a prayer group, a parish, a religious community, the diocese, or in the universal church. Even people with strong and effective charisms are not enough. Only leaders who are docile to the Spirit and to his counsels can successfully guide his people.

Knowledge

Knowledge is the gift of the Holy Spirit that produces in us a deep trust and sureness about the Lord and the truths

of Christian revelation. It is traditionally viewed as the perfection of the virtue of faith. When we speak of the release
of the Spirit enabling us not just to believe things about the
Lord but to know him personally and to know that what he
says is true, we are speaking of having received the gift of
knowledge.

Knowledge is a gift that is not only noticeable within
ourselves, but is also noticeable to those around us. When
people see the sureness and strength of our newly acquired
Spirit-filled faith (which is a manifestation of knowledge),
they tend to react strongly and often negatively. Comments
like "How can they be so sure of what they believe?" and
"Do they think they have a direct pipeline to God?" are
typical negative responses people make after talking to charismatics who are newly baptized in the Spirit.

The gift of knowledge plays a key role in the initial phase
of life in the Spirit. It gives us sure and solid ground to
stand on as we enter into a spiritual life-style which is, in
many ways, unlike anything we have ever experienced before.
If it were not for the strong knowledge the Lord gives us
that we are being led by him in our new life, we would
quickly become confused and perhaps retreat from the path
he has placed us on.

The main way the Lord fosters the gift of knowledge
among charismatics is by teaching us to live by expectant
faith. Expectant faith is a faith by which we not only know
that things are true, but also one by which we accomplish
things in the Lord. It is one of the hallmarks of charismatic
life. Through it, we are able to claim healings, work miracles,
have our prayers answered, prophesy, speak in tongues
and perform many other powerful works that are part of the
charismatic experience. When we claim things in faith, ex-
pecting to receive them because of the Lord's promises in
the scriptures, and then when we actually do receive what
we have asked for, our faith in the Lord is built up and
perfected. This leads us to have a more mature knowledge
of him.

However, as we grow more expectant in faith and in
knowledge, we must be careful to avoid the tendency to
develop mismatched expectations as to how to use these

powerful gifts the Lord has given us. As we pray for healings and other favors with expectant faith, we must retain
an openness to having our prayers answered in a way that
is different from what we had hoped for. When we claim in
faith victory over some obstacle in our lives in Christ, and
the victory does not seem to come, we need to be ready to
adjust our perspective on how the Lord wants us to gain
victory over that obstacle. We must not use the principle of
claiming things in expectant faith to try to gain control over
God's plans. As we balance our practice of expectant faith
with our openness to the Lord teaching us new ways to
grow in faith, we will be in a position that allows for a
steady increase of the gift of knowledge.

Understanding

Understanding is traditionally defined as the gift of the
Spirit which enlightens our minds and hearts with divine
truth so that we can grasp the mysteries of the Lord. Increased depth in personal prayer, a new ability to penetrate
the meaning of the scriptures, and a deepened appreciation
of the sacraments—all of which are commonly experienced
after being baptized in the Spirit—are manifestations of this
gift.

Several other charismatic graces are caused by the outpouring of the gift of understanding. Understanding enables us to appreciate the gift of tongues, which from the
standpoint of human reason makes no sense. On a broader
level, understanding makes us able to grasp the meaning of
the whole charismatic experience. How often do we find it
difficult to explain to others what the baptism in the Spirit
is, or how wonderful a prayer meeting is. We usually end
our explanations by telling them to "come and see," or by
saying "you have to experience it." The reason we can't
fully explain our experience is that, humanly speaking, it
can't be done. We can say all we want about why tongues is
important, how prophecy is really what the Lord is saying,
etc., but only the Spirit himself, through imparting the gift

of understanding, can confirm in our minds and hearts what is happening.

Unlike some of the other Isaiah gifts we have been considering, understanding usually stays with charismatics strongly throughout life in the Spirit. Even after several years of involvement in the charismatic renewal, though many persons might be less open to things such as words of counsel or praying with expectant faith, most people still maintain their initial graces of drawing insight from scripture, deeper sacramental lives, and rich personal prayer lives. However, growth in this gift is often stifled, and understanding may even weaken as time goes on.

Two tendencies lie beneath this difficulty. The first follows from the fact that the initial experience of understanding is so sudden and powerful. The day before we were filled with the Spirit we may, for example, have read scripture with no spiritual insight, while, literally one day later, we might have read it with a powerful sense of insight. This experience of understanding might be at a depth which would normally take a person many years of effort to achieve. Such an experience does not point very clearly to a dimension of growth in this gift. In fact, it can actually make us think the opposite, i.e., that we have come, by some special movement of the Spirit, to full maturity in spiritual insight and have no need of further growth.

The second tendency is one in which we unconsciously adopt a spirituality oriented too far in the direction of evangelical revivalism, believing that, once we are saved, filled and delivered, we become instant saints. We end up spending most of our time reviving those spiritual moments in our lives and have little else to offer to those who want to be filled with the Spirit.

As a counter to these tendencies, we must learn to integrate our vision of how understanding operates in us into traditional church teaching on the interior life. Doing this will help teach us how we can grow in this gift.

The "interior life" is the traditional name given to our ongoing personal relationship with the Lord, with a special emphasis on our prayer lives. There are three general stages in the interior life: the purgative, the illuminative and the unitive stages. A major goal in the interior life is the attainment of the gift of understanding and consequent growth in it. This is brought about, according to Catholic tradition, by purging oneself of vice and growing in virtue until one comes to a spiritual point at which the Lord begins to illumine the mind supernaturally with his truth.

In the charismatic renewal, participants normally begin their interior lives by experiencing some aspects of the illuminative stage. For example, the baptism in the Spirit has been defined by some spiritual theologians as infused contemplation or as simplified prayer, which are marks of the illuminative stage, as is the ability to penetrate the deeper meaning of scripture mentioned above.

To achieve a sense of growth and of the progressive stages of the spiritual life, charismatics must look back, so to speak, to the purgative stage and involve themselves in it. The purgative stage is the time during which we cooperate with the Lord in overcoming the sinful habits which cloud our souls and obscure our vision of the Lord. As we apply ourselves to the tasks of this stage, we must first acknowledge that we are still sinful in many ways, no matter how deep our repentence was when we received the Spirit or how lofty and illuminative our experiences of him have been. If we do not admit this to ourselves, it will be impossible for us to sort out the roots of our sinfulness so that we can begin to purify our souls.

Once we understand in our heart that we are in need of purification, we can look to a variety of ways of examining ourselves so as to locate specific areas that need work. The traditional practice of examining one's conscience according to a set of norms, such as the Ten Commandments, the Beatitudes, the fruit of the Spirit, the cardinal and theological virtues, or the seven capital sins, can be of great value in the purgative process. Much of the literature of Catholic spirituality has as its purpose coming to a firm grasp of how to apply these various norms successfully. Exposure to this literature, with the assistance of someone more mature in Christ, should be a normal part of growing in the gift of understanding.

Wisdom

We possess the gift of wisdom when we become able to make true judgments about everything in our lives on the basis of a deep, personal union with the Lord in love. The "spiritual man" of 1 Cor. 2:15 who "judges all things" is the person who has attained the gift of wisdom. Having lived the Christian life wholeheartedly, in spite of all its trials and difficulties, this person has been brought by the Spirit to the point where he or she has a supernatural ability to know how life should be lived so that the Lord's will is perfectly accomplished. This person judges correctly about all things in life, whether they concern practical, day-to-day issues or lofty, mystical truths.

Wisdom is coupled with the virtue of love in traditional spirituality. It is seen as the highest kind of love—what love looks like when it has been perfected and supernaturalized by the full presence of the Spirit in the soul. Although we don't experience what we would term "wisdom" when we first come into life in the Spirit, we do experience a strong outpouring of the gift of love. So, as a way of discussing the gift of wisdom in charismatic life, let us examine the way the Spirit increases our love when we are filled with the Spirit.

When we are baptized in the Spirit, we normally sense that we have been given a greater love of the Lord and of other persons. Outsiders often comment that persons who become filled with the Spirit grow more compassionate and are more pleasant to be around. Those of us who found it difficult to express our love emotionally feel a greater emotional freedom in our relationships with others. Doing things for others seems to come easier to us. The burdensome aspect of self-sacrifice seems to leave us (at least for a while). We feel more free to be ourselves. We are less constrained to act according to set rules of behavior in a formalistic way. In general, we experience a tremendous sense of having grown in love, or perhaps having discovered for the first time what it means to love. We feel that so many walls, between ourselves and the Lord and other persons, have been torn down. Our hearts seem less made of stone and more made of flesh. This outpouring of love is correctly viewed as an initial manifestation of the gift of wisdom.

How can we as charismatics grow in love so that we can grow in the gift of wisdom? One thing we can do is to take the key aspects of our initial experience of Spirit-filled love and build on them. The "first love" of the baptism in the Spirit is emotional, easy, spontaneous and self-expressive. If we complement these aspects of love with some traditional wisdom on the nature of love, we will see a path we can follow as we strive to grow in wisdom.

The good feelings we experience are often dismissed as emotionalism. Though this problem can develop if we don't establish a solid spiritual foundation for our initial feelings, the Lord's purpose in giving them is to begin to increase our heartfelt fervor for following him. Tradition calls this fervor the "affective" dimension of love. It teaches that there are two basic components of love—the effective part (our behavior) and the affective (heartfelt fervor) part. The affective part is more important, though both parts are essential to loving. Rightly responded to, our good feelings about the Lord and others will be the beginning of an ever-deepening desire to do God's will, and will more and more involve, not only our emotions, but our whole hearts (including our wills).

The sense of ease which accompanies our first love needs to be complemented with the understanding that Christian love is normally hard work and that, when the initial grace passes, loving others will be as hard as it ever was. To love means to serve others, to forget about oneself, and is usually accompanied by suffering and at least some measure of rejection. Love is made more difficult by our tendency toward sloth (sorrow at the prospect of loving the Lord and others) and self-centeredness. Love seems easier at first because of our sense of zeal at beginning a new and great work. (In the context of religious movements, this is called "first fervor.") As we settle into the long-term task of love, and the initial zeal wears off, we must constantly fight sloth and self-centeredness, while resting more in the abiding joy and peace of the Lord which will accompany our life of trial and suffering.

The spontaneity of our first love is experienced as a liberation from an approach to the Christian life which is legalistic and rule-oriented. This liberty must be protected. However, having this sense of liberation can lead to a reaction against such practices as making commitments, vows, promises. When seen in the proper perspective, such practices are foundational to growth in love. God himself, throughout scripture, loves us by making commitments to us and keeping them. In establishing a good pattern for growth in love, we must always view the two principles of freedom and commitment as complementary to each other and as building on each other—not as opposed to each other.

The freedom of self-expression which accompanies the baptism in the Spirit is of great spiritual and psychological value. Much of the lack of love in our society arises out of fear of what others will think or do if we let our real selves be known. It goes without saying that overcoming this fear is a step in the right direction. However, being honest or uninhibited does not automatically mean that we are being more loving. We must complement our freedom of self-expression with the "putting on of Christ," so that we will reflect Christ and not just ourselves. As we focus our hearts on the re-creation of our character in Christ's image, which he communicates to us in prayer, the scriptures and our brothers and sisters, the Lord will gradually remake us into the persons we were meant to be.

As we continue to grow in the virtue of love, we will come to a point where our loving begins to seem to us to be God loving in and through us more than us consciously and deliberately doing the work. Our hearts will be closer to God's heart. Our minds will do less thinking about how to love. Our wills will decide to love more quickly. Our love will bear more fruit. We will do "just the right thing" more often than before. We will have a greater capacity for self-sacrifice. Others will seek us out more often as a source of good judgment. All these things are indicators of the growth of wisdom in our lives.

When we become mature in the gift of wisdom, we will

have attained the highest earthly goal of the Christian. We will habitually possess ". . . a spirit that is intelligent, holy . . . pure, loving the good, beneficent, humane, steadfast . . . overseeing all, and penetrating through all spirits" (Wis. 7:22).

CHAPTER 3:

The Sacraments

From the beginning of the charismatic renewal, there has been considerable focus on how life in the Spirit relates to the sacraments. There are several reasons for this. One obvious reason is that the label given the initial experience—*baptism* in the Spirit—confuses outsiders. Participants in the renewal have continually found it necessary to explain to others that this label does not point to a new sacrament, or to rebaptism, but is a reference to a passage in Acts 1 about the experience of Pentecost. The typical explanation goes on to talk about how the baptism in the Spirit, viewed from the standpoint of the sacraments, is an activation of the graces we receive at Baptism and Confirmation.

Another reason for this focus is the need felt by those involved in the renewal to defend it against detractors who see it as driving people away from the sacraments. The baptism in the Spirit does not draw people away from sacramental life, their argument goes, but actually draws them back to the sacraments with a stronger appreciation of them.

There is a third reason behind the charismatic tendency to

focus on its relationship to sacramental life. Just as many
Protestants tend to view their life of grace in terms of scripture and personal experience, there is a traditional belief
among Catholics that one's life of grace is ministered principally through the sacraments. (This belief refers to "habitual"
or "sanctifying" grace in one's life, which are the Catholic
terms for the principle way the Lord dispenses grace. Catholic thought also talks about "actual" graces that are given to
deal with specific situations.) Therefore, a grace-filled experience such as life in the Spirit automatically calls for a sacramental interpretation in their minds. For example, such
persons would continually feel the need to see their new
closeness to the Lord as having Eucharistic implications, or
their new strength and power in the Spirit as somehow
linked to their reception of Confirmation.

It is along the lines of this third reason for linking the
charismatic experience with the sacraments that I would like
our discussion to proceed. I want to take this direction
because it is right for us as Catholics to see our lives of grace
and faith as principally mediated, if not directly then at least
indirectly, through the seven sacraments and through the
ministry of the word. (Vatican II states that this is brought
about principally through "the ministry of the word and of
the sacraments."* When we become filled with the Spirit,
we come to know experientially that the Lord imparts greater
faith through the scriptures. Sometimes, however, we tend
to forget our roots in the grace of the sacraments. Although
some might feel that their experience of them is enriched,
others tend to drift toward a mentality which sees life in
Christ mainly in terms of appropriating the word of God in
scripture and meeting the Lord in experience. This mentality can cause us to think, for example, that our sacramental
baptism was not effective, while our Spirit-baptism was. Or
it can lead us to think that Mass and Communion are
meaningful only when we attend with charismatic friends.
Or we may think that the Anointing of the Sick is only
efficacious when ministered with enlivened and Spirit-filled
faith. Some who unwittingly adopt such a mentality eventu-

*Decree on the Laity, 6.

ally come to a point where the whole notion of seven sacraments seems to them some kind of medieval construct of the church. After all, they think, didn't Jesus really institute only two sacraments, Baptism and Eucharist, as many non-Catholics believe?

Often this mistaken approach is an overreaction to the position which says that the only way a Catholic can view life in Christ is in terms of the sacraments, to the detriment of scripture and personal experience. This position, which was quite prevalent before the council, is still held by many traditional Catholics I know. If I use too much scripture or talk too much about personal experience when we are discussing a religious topic, they become suspicious of my "Protestant leanings." But, when I talk in terms of *sacramental* graces, their faces light up!

Others adopt it because their prior experience of the sacraments seemed fruitless and ineffective.

Still others argue that, since the council speaks of the church as sacrament, we should no longer look at the sacraments according to the old theology, according to which they were the seven principle channels of sanctifying grace. These persons misunderstand the intent of the council. The new theological statements about the church as a sacrament are enrichments of church teaching, but they are meant to be integrated into the traditional framework.

Whatever our reasons might be for abandoning or minimalizing Catholic sacramental teaching, we charismatics must repent and open our minds to understanding how the Lord works through the seven sacraments in our lives. We will then see that the grace imparted in the baptism in the Spirit is meant to *enrich* our experience of the sacraments. When we appreciate this, we will have a more balanced and truly Catholic understanding of life in the Spirit.

Let us proceed to a consideration of how each sacrament is enriched in charismatic life. Since I am not a theologian or expert in the area, I will offer my personal reflections on the matter. One might call what follows my personal testimony on how I grew in appreciation of the sacraments after being filled with the Spirit. I believe that my experience is fairly typical: in relating it, I hope to shed some light on the experience of the reader.

Rather than following the traditional Catholic order in which the sacraments are treated,* I will share about each sacrament in the order in which the Lord enriched my vision of that sacrament. He began by teaching me about Confirmation, then Baptism, Anointing of the Sick, Reconciliation, Eucharist, Matrimony and Holy Orders.

Confirmation

Confirmation is that sacrament whereby we are given a new strength, vigor and power to live for Christ and build his kingdom. Traditional Catholic teaching told us that this sacrament filled us with the seven gifts of the Holy Ghost and enabled us to become new soldiers of Jesus Christ. When I received Confirmation as a child, my main concern was how hard the bishop would hit me on the cheek (a part of the ritual no longer practiced). I did not have much of a sense that this event would "confirm"—strengthen—me as a Catholic. But I remember that it did give me new strength. I knew that something had happened to me spiritually, and afterward I seemed to approach my life as a Catholic more seriously, at least for a while.

As my life went on, the grace of this sacrament, as manifested in the seven Isaiah gifts, was at work in me, although I was seldom conscious of it. Many times, when I needed special wisdom or counsel to get through a difficult situation, the Lord provided it. At other stressful times, I was able to draw on special faith and courage in ways that would not have been possible without the sacrament of Confirmation.

When I was prayed with to be baptized in the Spirit, I began to experience the charismatic gifts, which are traditionally associated with Confirmation, but which had not been emphasized until the council and the advent of the renewal. Having been trained to view my life in terms of

*Baptism, Confirmation, Eucharist, Penance, Extreme Unction, Holy Orders, Matrimony.

sacramental graces, I looked at my experience as a fulfillment of my reception of Confirmation.

What I had formerly viewed as a kind of Catholic "rite of passage," similar to a Jewish bar-mitzvah, became an ongoing and powerful action of the Lord in my life. From time to time, leaders would speak of the need to be continually baptized in the Spirit. I interpreted this as meaning that we should make the grace of Confirmation a continuing reality in our lives.

I also gradually noticed that the seven gifts traditionally associated with the reception of Confirmation were stirred up and enhanced by the release of the Spirit. I sensed a new reverence and awe in God's presence. I had a new strength to go on. I had a deeper awareness of God as my Father. He gave me more ongoing counsel in my life. My increased faith gave me a stronger knowledge of him. Understanding of his mysteries was deepened, especially with regard to scripture. He gave me wisdom on how to love better.

As I look back now on what I have learned about the meaning of Confirmation, I can see three ways in which the Lord corrected my old view and enriched my life in him by giving me a new mentality with respect to this sacrament. First, he taught me that Confirmation was not just a religious event that was part of my past, but that it is meant to have ongoing significance in my daily life. As mentioned above, what is labeled by some as the process of being continually baptized in the Spirit can also be viewed as the Lord continually increasing in us the grace of Confirmation. Second, I have come to see that the sacrament of Confirmation is meant to pervade our whole spiritual life. It strengthens us on the level of our personalities, through the bestowal of the seven gifts, and on the level of our function in Christ's body through the bestowal of the different charisms. Third, I have come to see that the grace of the sacrament, though it is given at one moment, is meant to unfold gradually in our lives as we grow spiritually in the use of the seven gifts and the charisms. There is, as traditional theological expression teaches, an indelible mark conferred on the soul by Confirmation. We cannot receive it over and over

again. But its effects in us are largely latent when we receive
it, and only with time does the full impact of this sacrament
become evident.

Baptism

Baptism is the sacrament through which we receive the
Lord into our hearts and are initiated into the life of grace
(life in the Spirit), becoming children of God and heirs of
heaven. The baptism in the Spirit, in so far as it involves
accepting the Lord as our personal Savior or committing
ourselves to following him more seriously, involves a release of Baptismal grace.

I was somewhat committed to following the Lord prior to
being prayed with, but did not have a close, personal relationship with him. Like most Catholics, I was baptized as an
infant and grew up never having made a conscious decision
to follow Christ. Nevertheless, I was committed to follow
him and I tried to live out my commitment. The grace of
Baptism was operative in my life even though my parents
and godparents were the initial agents of my commitment.

Still, there was something incomplete about my understanding of what it meant to be under the lordship of Jesus
through my baptismal covenant with him. I remember
thinking, as I renewed my baptismal promises each year on
Holy Saturday along with the rest of the Catholic Church,
how important and meaningful an event Baptism is. I also
felt this when I witnessed adult baptisms. But I sensed at
the same time that I had not experienced in a personal way
the full impact of this sacrament. Many of the phrases used
in the Baptismal liturgy, such as "sonship with God" or
"liberation from sin and death," seemed in my mind to be
more rhetorical statements than realities.

Then, when I was filled with the Spirit, all the baptismal
promises made by the Lord to those who accept him came
alive in my life. I felt free. I felt born again. I had a sense of
having been adopted. I felt forgiven. I experienced myself
as a new creation—a new man. The Lord had broken through
whatever it was in my heart that had kept the graces given

me at Baptism from being fully realized. A little later on, through experiencing deliverance from evil spirits, I learned to recognize and fight against demonic temptations, and thus was freed from any unconscious influence of the devil— something which is another intended effect of sacramental Baptism. All the grace which was mine to claim because of my infant Baptism became actualized when I was prayed with. Since I was now aware of the Lord keeping his part of our (his and my) baptismal covenant, I was stirred up to make a fuller commitment to following him. In making this fuller commitment, I had recovered for myself the meaning of Baptism, both in terms of its rewards and responsibilities.

Today my baptismal covenant with God, enriched by my charismatic experience, is more than ever the foundation of all that I am and do. Jesus is my Lord. I want to know, love and serve God here on earth and be with him forever in heaven. In other words, I want to live according to the grace of the sacrament of Baptism.

The Anointing of the Sick

Witnessing the miraculous healing power of the Lord was the most exciting part of my initial experience of life in the Spirit. At the first national conference at Notre Dame in 1967, two participants prayed over a man who had just been hit by a car, and he was instantly healed. Events such as this one, which I had previously thought occurred only at Lourdes and in the lives of great saints, became common-place in my life and in the lives of others who were involved in the renewal. At the time, we did not associate our experiences with the Anointing of the Sick. Church teaching on the sacrament was then in a state of transition. The notion of "Extreme Unction," still prevalent at that time, called forth images of the soul being prepared for death, rather than of the body and soul being healed.

As my prayer group continued to exercise and experiment with the gift of healing, the Lord gave us greater understanding of how to use this powerful charism. At the same time, in the universal church, he was enriching understanding of the sacrament of the sick, not only regarding its use when death was near, but also as a means of reviving the New Testament practice of praying with persons for spiritual and physical healings whenever it was appropriate. Clearly the Lord was preparing his church, both at the grass-roots level and at the level of the magisterium, for an increase of his healing power in the world.

At our grass-roots level, the Lord first taught us that we should pray for healing often—whenever someone was in need. He did this to counteract our traditional Catholic tendency to suffer through all our illnesses and physical discomfort, offering them up for the souls in purgatory, rather than praying for healing from them. Sometimes we prayed for healing and those we prayed with were not immediately healed. At these times, God taught us that perhaps we were not exercising enough expectant faith in our prayer, or that we needed to pray for an extended period of time with fasting as part of our effort. He also showed us that some persons had a special charism for healing. Thus, more people would be healed if they received the ministry of a person with the charism of healing. He showed us that physical ailments are often caused by underlying spiritual problems. Many persons were healed after they had repented from their sins or were delivered from the influence of an evil spirit. He showed us that inner spiritual healing was just as important as physical healing, and that we should pray for these kinds of healings as well as physical healings. Finally, he taught us (again) that some physical suffering was allowed by him so that a person could endure it patiently for his own spiritual benefit and for that of others, including the souls in purgatory.

At the same time, in the wider church, ministers of the sacrament of the sick were given greater freedom to pray with and anoint those who were ill, whether or not they were near death. Many priests, especially charismatic priests, began to hold parish healing services, where they administered the sacrament to those who needed it. Thus, even outside the renewal, there was an increase of physical and spiritual healing in the church.

As the Anointing of the Sick became a more common practice among Catholics, I began to understand how the Lord was enriching the Catholic attitude toward the sacrament of the sick through charismatic healing. Although charismatic healing is perhaps more an actual grace than a habitual grace flowing from the sacrament, its powerful effects and its frequent use have strengthened the faith of the church in the reality of healing power in the sacrament of the sick and caused her to use this sacrament more frequently.

Healing in the Christian life is not meant by God to be something extraordinary, manifested only in the lives of great saints or in times of revival. The Lord has always desired that healing be a normal part of our lives. Since the council, he has used both the charismatic renewal and an enriched theological understanding of the sacrament of the sick to make this clear.

Reconciliation

Growth in forgiveness is one of the most fruitful aspects of life in the Spirit. As we are baptized in the Spirit, the Lord enables us to seek and receive forgiveness from him in a deeper way. Also, he leads us to seek and receive forgiveness from one another in ways that are more practical and real than before.

While I was growing up I had notions of repentance and forgiveness that were centered mainly around my relationship with God. I can remember only a few instances prior to the release of the Spirit when I actually asked someone other than the Lord to forgive me. Even when I asked God for forgiveness, it was usually because I had broken one of the rules he gave me to follow. I didn't normally think of my sins as hurting or offending God personally, though I was taught that I should feel such sentiments.

Nevertheless, the Lord worked powerfully with me through the sacrament of Penance, as it was called then. I received it regularly—often once a week. Beforehand I would examine my conscience according to the rules I had been taught. I remember experiencing real remorse and shame as I entered the confessional and then, after having received the sacrament, experiencing great joy, peace and relief. These feelings were not the result of some kind of psychological catharsis. A real spiritual power was present that had not been there before. I experienced new strength in dealing with temptation. All this led me to a strong belief in the reality of an immediate sacramental grace that the Lord gives when the sacrament is administered.

When I was filled with the Spirit, I experienced enrichment in my attitude toward repentance and forgiveness in three ways. I have always viewed these enrichments as ways the Lord has taught me how better to respond to the grace which flows from the sacrament of Reconciliation.

The first enrichment involved a change in my heart attitude from imperfect to perfect contrition. For me, the baptism in the Spirit was, among other things, a revelation of the goodness of God. The Lord "moved in" to my heart and began to dwell there more fully than before. His lovingkindness, mercy, goodness, etc., were much more evident to me. I could not help but change my attitude toward sins from one which focused on how they hurt my situation to viewing them as offending my all-loving, all-merciful Creator, Redeemer and Sustainer. It goes without saying that this change of heart produced in me a deeper spirit of repentance and empowered me to overcome sins which previously had seemed too difficult or not important enough to deal with.

My consciousness of the need for reconciliation with persons I had wronged was also enriched by my charismatic experience. The Spirit first led me to a new understanding of how it is that Christians must be brothers and sisters, not only on the level of the Mystical Body of Christ, but on the level of our real, practical lives. I was given a thirst for greater unity with other Christians. I set myself against obstacles to that unity, which are the sins we commit against one another in daily living together.

At this point, I discovered a better way to examine my conscience. Previously, I had been concerned with not lying, cheating, being lustful or greedy, etc. This was the way I had examined my conscience as a child, according to the 10 Commandments. Now I also had to examine myself in more subtle areas of personal relationships, such as how I acted with respect to gentleness and kindness; whether I acted out of bitterness, resentment, envy; how merciful and gracious I was, and so on. I learned gradually that the deeper blocks to union with God and other persons are overcome, not simply by obeying clear rules—though this must be done as a minimum requirement—but by engaging in the more complex task of growth in charity and overcoming hidden vices.

Though my conscience (and my consciousness) had been enriched with new ways to overcome sins against others, I still was deficient in repairing the wrongs I had done. If I had been unkind or had failed in charity, I could confess it sacramentally, but how could I patch things up with the person I had offended? Sound teaching on this matter surfaced early in the history of the renewal. The content of the teaching runs as follows: If you have wronged someone, you can repair the situation by directly asking the offended person to forgive you, assuming that he or she is of a mind to forgive you. You should admit without rationalizations that you were wrong and want to change. If you are on the other side in these situations—if you have been wronged— then you must be open to the one who wronged you and forgive him or her as God continually forgives you.

Eucharist

The Eucharist is the source and summit, the sum and substance of the Christian life. It is the sacrament which binds all the others together and binds us to the Lord and to one another, just as love is the sum of all virtues, and wisdom is the sum of all gifts of the Spirit. As Leo XIII taught in his encyclical *Mirae Caritatis*, "Indeed, in the Eucharist alone are contained, in a remarkable richness and variety of miracles, all supernatural realities."

As a youth, I continually clung to the Eucharist. Even when nothing else was clear about my life—where I was going, what was the best way to be—I could always rest on Holy Communion as a base of stability in the midst of turmoil. I believe that my experience was typical of those who receive the Eucharist regularly, not because of any merit on our part, but because of the infinite generosity of our Lord in the sacrament.

Life in the Spirit made me more aware of the communal implications of Communion. As was the case with most Catholics, my reception of the Eucharist had been largely a private matter between myself and God. Some of the changes in the liturgy instituted by the council began to change my perspective, but I still fundamentally saw Communion as God ministering to me individually.

During the handshake of peace at a Mass I attended about a week after being filled with the Spirit, I suddenly became acutely aware of all the other people there, and became uncomfortable, confused and distracted. I asked the Lord afterward what was going on. Was it a spiritual attack? Was the liturgy being conducted wrongly? Did I have a case of indigestion? The Lord didn't answer, except to say that I should remember the event. Later on, I realized that the incident marked the beginning of the Lord's efforts to free me from my individualistic piety, so that he could fill me with a more communal, and thus more authentically Christian approach to receiving his Body and Blood.

As I continued in my charismatic life, I became increasingly involved in a covenant Christian community. The Lord gradually enriched my attitude toward the Eucharist in this context so that I began to understand Communion as producing community, as being the result of community, and as being the celebration of community. My enriched awareness developed in a covenant community setting, but I believe the Lord teaches people the same things in prayer groups, even when they are only loosely committed.

As he was cultivating a sense in me of the communal nature of the Eucharist, the Lord also began to fill me with a deeper sense of how he imparts his own divine life when we receive him. He taught me a deeper meaning of the word "life" in the passage, "unless you eat the flesh of the Son of Man and drink his blood, you have no life in you"

(John 6:53). This life is not just fuller human life, or even the ability to live Christianity in a better way. It is the divine and eternal essence of God himself that is offered every time we approach the altar to eat the bread and drink from the cup.

The Lord also gave me new insight into the Eucharist as "the source and summit of all evangelization."* My strength and zeal to spread the gospel came from reading scripture and personal prayer, but also from receiving Communion. The Eucharist seemed to light a fire in my heart to tell people about the Lord. I also began to discover the importance of evangelizing persons, not only to a personal relationship with Christ in prayer, but also to an embracing of sacramental life, which culminates in the reception of Communion. This was especially true with respect to leading lapsed Catholics back to the Lord. Their return to Christ never seemed complete until they began again (or perhaps for the first time) to receive the Body and Blood of Christ with faith and devotion.

Matrimony

Since I am not married, my reflections on the work of the Spirit in this sacrament will be offered from a distance. Still, God does so much to enrich marriages through the charismatic experience that the fruit of his work is very clear, even to those who have not yet received this sacrament.

As a single person, I was ministered to by the sacrament of Matrimony because I was raised by parents who were dedicated Catholics. I witnessed their matrimonial lives on a daily basis, both in terms of their relationship with each other and the way they raised me and my brother and sisters. The overriding goal of my family was growth in Christ. My parents were active in their parish. They both seemed to be members of most of the organizations set up by the parish. They sent us to Catholic schools, upheld Catholic teaching at home, had us pray the rosary together,

*Decree on Missions, 9.

and so on. Our family life was full of Christian ideals.

However, we did not share Christ outwardly with one another. Our Christian family life was one of discipline without the excitement that one comes to expect from life in the Spirit. As we grew older, the forces of secularism in American culture began to exert a negative influence on our family life together.

I was no longer living with my family when I was baptized in the Spirit, but most members of my prayer group were married persons, and, as we shared more of our lives with one another, I began to see how the Lord was ministering to their marriages.

Like my parents, some of the couples had strong and stable Christian marriages. Unlike my family, however, Christ was openly shared and glorified in their families, and their children had close personal relationships with the Lord. Other marriages seemed to be on more shaky ground. But the sharing of the Lord in these marriages made them much stronger than they would have been otherwise.

In spite of having richer fellowship in Christ because of their Spirit-filled life, all the couples experienced growing pressure on their families from the same secular forces which had affected my family as I was growing up. Jobs were calling for more time; the media were calling them and their children to immorality; and the church did not seem to offer much help. Their lives were under seige from all sides and they had nowhere to turn.

Then the Spirit moved in power. He began to enrich matrimonial life among charismatics in a way that dealt with many of the problems just described.

The first thing the Lord did was to strengthen the meaning of the marriage covenant. The experience of the release of the Spirit fortified couples' belief in their marriage commitment to each other by giving them a greater awareness of how their covenant in Baptism made them, first of all, brother and sister in Christ. This deeper realization of their baptismal union in Christ gave their marriages a firmer foundation; it was now easier to deal with the stresses and strains of married life. Thus, even during periods when they weren't getting along well as husband and wife, Spirit-filled couples could find stability in their more important role as Christians—to raise their family in Christ and to function in the body of Christ according to their charisms.

Another area enriched by the Lord was sexuality. The Spirit moved in and through the renewal to reaffirm and clarify traditional Christian teaching on sexual purity, in order that all Christians, including married persons, would become better able to embrace God's truth about sexuality with strength and assurance. This gave them greater ability to maintain their integrity as men and women in contemporary society, where the truth about sexuality is constantly under attack.

Through the release of the Spirit, the Lord also taught couples and families that they must minister to one another if they were to succeed in overcoming the current obstacles to Christian family living. The sacrament of Matrimony was never meant to be lived out by each family on its own without help from others. Families, as the basic social units of the church, must be connected with one another for Matrimony to have its full effect in corporate church life. This became clear to married couples as they committed more of their lives to each other. Before this commitment, the Lord had certainly moved them forward in their marriages, but something was lacking. When they committed themselves to one another, becoming a "family of families," the Spirit was able to restore Christian family life fully.

Holy Orders

This is another sacrament I have not received, but I feel qualified to offer some reflections on how life in the Spirit enriches Orders because I have witnessed these enrichments in the lives of many charismatic friends who are priests. Also, Orders is a sacrament especially of ministry to others, and I have been directly affected by it in the same way that I was affected by the matrimonial ministry of my parents.

The persons whose religious lives made the deepest impression on me as a child were priests. This was typical, at least for men, in preconciliar Catholic life. The priesthood was a ministry which called on the priest to set himself apart as "another Christ" to his people and to society as a whole.

All this seemed to change during the first years of the conciliar era. Priests began to mix more with the laity and share more of their concerns. Their self-image of being Christ to society seemed to become less clear in their minds. Some became personally confused and unsure about their calling. Many of them left the priesthood. Many others who remained seemed to have lost their sense of mission. The traditional image of the priest as "another Christ" was no longer dominant in the attitudes of laity as well as clergy. Priests who clung to the old heroic ideal were often scorned as hypocrites or dismissed as vestiges of a bygone era.

In the midst of this situation, many priests and laypersons were filled with the Spirit. Both priestly and lay awareness of the meaning of Orders was immediately enriched, though in an indirect way, because priests and laypersons felt closer to one another as persons. Priests saw the laity as more fully committed to Christ than before and the laity saw priests as more human and approachable. This experience of rapprochement between clergy and laity laid the groundwork for other enrichments.

Priests soon developed a new sense of their charisms as apostles, prophets, pastors, teachers and evangelists (Eph. 4:11). Priests are assumed to have received these foundational charisms at their ordination, but the actual manifestation of them was often lacking in priestly ministry to one degree or another. Life in the Spirit seemed to awaken gifts of leadership in the ministry of many priests. Their sense of having an apostolic mission to build their parishes was activated. Their call to speak the Lord's word, including some of its more challenging prophetic aspects, became stronger. Their sense of having a flock which needed them as pastors and guides grew in their hearts. They saw in a clearer way the need for teaching in many areas of the Christian life. They experienced a new ability to preach and evangelize others.

Priests also recovered a sense of the priesthood as mainly a spiritual, as opposed to a secular or temporal ministry. This enrichment was actually a recovery of a preconciliar insight into the nature of Holy Orders which was being neglected by many priests in the conciliar era in favor of political, cultural, social and economic interests. The council views these interests, which are in the temporal order, as mainly the concern of the laity. In spite of this teaching, some priests have drifted toward secular (nonsacred, temporal) involvements, partly because these areas seemed to afford more opportunities for serving mankind effectively, and partly because the possibilities for spiritual ministry seemed to be drying up. However, when the charismatic dimension is added to spiritual ministry, it comes alive again and actually emerges as a more powerful way to spread the gospel than working in the temporal and secular arena.

Another charismatic enrichment of Orders has been the development of the renewal as a resource for new clergy, especially permanent deacons. Many men who became involved in the renewal gradually developed strong ministry gifts. For some of them, these gifts became the starting point for a call to the priesthood or the diaconate.

In addition to acting as a spiritual catalyst for vocations to the clergy, the renewal is an excellent setting for those who have vocations to grow in their ministry skills. A man who goes through the seminary or a deacon-training program after having been involved in the running of a prayer group is much better prepared to assume reponsibilities in areas of pastoral ministry than he would be without that experience.

Charismatic renewal also enriches Orders through its effects on the laypersons who rely on clergy for leadership. The release of the Spirit normally leads to the realization that authority can have a positive value in life. This runs counter to the prevailing modern sentiment, which views authority as, at best, a necessary evil. When laypersons enter into the charismatic experience in the right way, they accept the authority and Lordship of Jesus; they experience a release of power as they submit their lives to him. They then learn that submission includes submission to his will as manifested in the charisms he gives to his body. They begin to see how his will is clarified through the ministry of those who are leaders in the body. They are then led further to

the insight that the Lord has established institutional authority in his church, "to whose authority the Spirit subjects
even those endowed with charisms" (*Constitution on the
Church*, 7)—the pope, the bishops, and the priests and deacons representing the bishops. Charismatics begin to see
that the Lord also speaks authoritatively through these offices.
In short, one's appreciation of Orders is enriched as one
becomes aware of its governmental aspects, which charismatics come to see as valuable in discerning God's will for
their lives.

In this chapter, I have outlined how the charismatic experience enriched my sacramental life. I have also argued,
between the lines, that Spirit-filled Catholics should view
the life of grace as flowing from the sacraments as a principle source.

By way of ending the chapter, let me refer to a very
helpful explanation of how one can see life as a way of responding to the Lord in the grace of the seven sacraments.
It is found in the *Summa Theologica* (III, 65, 1). Aquinas's
analogy runs as follows: the spiritual life can be viewed as
unfolding in a way similar to bodily life. (Grace builds on
nature.) Bodily life unfolds on the level of the individual
and the community. On the individual level, the body is
born, has natural growth and nourishment, and a healing
growth when natural growth is impeded by illness or
accidents. The body must first come into existence—be born.
Baptism, by which we are reborn in Christ, corresponds to
this event. Second, the body grows naturally to maturity,
and this corresponds to Confirmation, which brings us to
spiritual maturity. Third, whether growing or fully mature,
the body needs ongoing nourishment, and this corresponds
to our spiritual food and drink, which is the Eucharist.

When illness or accident strikes, the body needs some
kind of remedy to get back to normal functioning. It needs
two things: first, a healing medicine or treatment, which
corresponds to Reconciliation, through which we are healed
of the disease of sin. It also needs a good diet and proper
exercise afterward. This is provided spiritually by the Anoint-

ing of the Sick, which has spiritual as well as physical revitalization and health as its purpose.

With regard to the human community, the expansion of mankind is assured by ruling and directing those already in existence, which spiritually corresponds to Orders, and by the bearing and raising of new persons, which corresponds to Matrimony.

St. Thomas and others have provided a number of explanations of how the sacraments impart grace to our whole lives as Christians. I mention this explanation because it has helped me come to a clearer understanding of the matter, and it serves as a good example of how the church, through the centuries, has instructed us about the sacraments.

CHAPTER 4:

Parish Life

Catholic life is normally lived out in the parish setting. It is only natural, then, that a common question for charismatic Catholics is, how does one fit the experience of life in the Spirit into parish life? The usual answer to this question is the formation of a parish prayer group. In this chapter we will consider the situation of parish prayer groups, past and present, and offer some suggestions as to what can happen to them in the future.

Some charismatics solve the problem of how to fit into their parishes by forming groups which are not parish-centered, while trying to act as a leaven within the parishes to which they belong. These groups are not as common as parish prayer groups, but they are often very large and powerful. For this reason, we will also discuss them in this chapter.

The main thesis of the chapter is that the Lord wants to use the charismatic experience, as it intersects Catholic parish life, to help implement his plan for greater lay participation in the renewal of the church. This plan is outlined in the council's *Decree on the Apostolate of Lay People (Apostolicam*

Actuositatem). The decree speaks of the need for laypersons to accept a call to an apostolate infinitely broader and more intense than in the past. New problems in the temporal order, involving a certain relinquishing of moral and spiritual values, seriously jeopardizing the Christian life, have arisen in our time. These must be addressed by an urgent and many-sided apostolate on the part of the laity. (AA1) Later, the decree paves the way for the charismatic renewal when it says:

> For the exercise of the apostolate, he (the Spirit) gives the faithful special gifts besides, "allotting to each as he wills" (I Cor. 12:11), so that each and all, putting at the service of others the gift received, may be "good stewards of God's varied gifts" (I Pet. 4:10), for the building up of the whole body in charity. From the reception of these charisms, even the most ordinary ones, there arises in the faithful the right and duty of exercising them in the Church and the world . . . in the freedom of the Holy Spirit . . . and in communion with their brothers and sisters in Christ and with their pastors especially (*Decree on the Laity*, 3).

Charismatics in the prayer group, full of the sense of giftedness called for in the *Decree on the Laity*, have been led by the Lord to the threshold of dealing with many of the "new problems" the decree speaks of. For the most part, however, they do not effectively deal with them. I believe that it is God's will that the church successfully address the new problems of today in parishes, and he wants the renewal to help lead the way by effectively addressing these problems as they arise in the lives of prayer group members who are in parishes.

Before addressing the main topics of this chapter, I would like to discuss three mistaken attitudes that many charismatics have with regard to parishes. The first is lack of appreciation for what the Lord has already done through the renewal to enliven parish life; the second is failure to recognize the value of the parish as an ongoing channel of grace; the third is a tendency to be blind to the spiritual value of the secular and cultural aspects of the parish.

Let me begin by sharing an experience I had recently while attending Mass at a parish which was unfamiliar to me.

As I entered the church, I noticed that there were several persons with guitars and flutes in the sanctuary who were preparing to lead the music for the Mass. I sat down in the pew and opened one of the songbooks. It was *Songs of Praise* from Servant Books, a charismatic publisher.

The opening song was "The Light of Christ," one of the most popular songs to come out of the renewal. I was pleasantly surprised at the vigor of the singing. When the celebrant began to lead the people in the prayers of the Mass in a free and enthusiastic manner, sprinkling his speech with phrases such as "Let's praise and thank the Lord for . . . ," and "Let's focus on Jesus now . . . ," I thought to myself that I must have stumbled on a charismatic parish. My suspicions were given greater weight during the sermon, which was a biblical call to seek a deep personal relationship with the Lord. Later in the Mass, it was announced that a healing Mass was scheduled in the coming month.

At the end of Mass, I asked someone whether, indeed, this was a charismatic parish and discovered that it was *not*. However, some parishioners were participants in a local prayer group, and one priest had attended a priest's conference in Steubenville and was marginally involved in the renewal. These persons had promoted a parish liturgical style in which people could worship in an atmosphere which was as lively and faith-building as the prayer-meeting atmosphere. The parish had not adopted all aspects of charismatic life, but it found the enlivened charismatic approach to liturgy so appealing that this became part of its life.

The experience gave me a clue to one way the Lord is working through the renewal to enliven parishes. Previously I had thought about this issue in the following way. The baptism in the Spirit is so powerful and so life-changing. Wouldn't it be great if every parishioner were filled with the

Spirit? Clergy and laity together would regularly use the spiritual gifts, would have fellowship and care for one another in real ways. . . . Why, the whole church would quickly be renewed! Why doesn't this happen? Why are so many people in the parishes resisting the work of the Lord?

On the other hand, I would think to myself, we charismatics aren't without our own problems in the area of resisting the Spirit, and maybe we aren't ready yet to share our insights with the rest of the body of Christ. Maybe this experience isn't for everyone; maybe we are a smaller-than-we-think part of a broad and complex move of God. We must guard against the charismatic tendency toward spiritual tunnel-vision.

But my experience taught me that I wasn't giving the Lord enough credit for what he has already done to enrich parishes through the renewal. I began to reflect on how Catholics in general are so much more open to physical and emotional healing than they were a few years ago. Priests in their sermons speak more freely about getting to know the Lord. Singing and the overall tone of worship at Mass seem to have more vitality. Intercession is taken more seriously. Spiritual warfare is given more credence. All these enrichments of the Catholic consciousness are in a large way effects of the charismatic renewal. We charismatics need to recognize and appreciate these enrichments and keep them in mind as we think and pray about our life in our parishes. If we don't, we will fall into the error of impatience with the Lord as he works on a broad level to renew the whole church.

Regarding the second mistaken attitude—our failure to recognize the value of the parish as an ongoing channel of grace—a story told me by Paul DeCelles, one of the founders of the renewal, helped to clarify my vision. He said that grace in the parish setting often operates like a subterranean river. It flows on the surface for a while, then goes underground, only to surface later on. He told me of a conversation with a friend of his who had just turned to the Lord. The man had grown up in a nominally Christian family. They had not practiced the faith in any evident way. He wasn't sure if he had been baptized a Catholic, but he sensed a deep love for the church welling up in his heart when he converted to Christ. The man did know, however, that his father was a baptized Catholic, and he sensed somehow that the Lord, in giving him a love for the church, was honoring the father's baptismal grace. As a way of giving image to the man's experience, DeCelles told him, "You may leave the church, but the church doesn't leave you."

Grace "like a subterranean river" is continually present in the parish, even when, on the surface, the parish may seem lifeless and unrenewed. We must accept and appreciate this truth if we are to understand how we can participate in the work of renewing our parishes.

The third mistaken attitude—demeaning the value of some of the less directly Christian aspects of parish life—is a particular problem for some persons who are new in the Spirit. They look at their past life in the parish, and focus on how it did not provide the kind of fellowship and support that they are now receiving from their charismatic friends. This often leads them to pass judgment on the aspects of their parish that are not "in the Spirit." What good is it, they think, to have parish dances and picnics, to have schools and PTAs that don't effectively transmit the gospel? Why have Mass on Sundays when the people there lack vitality in the Spirit? Why don't people start praying more? Why don't they seek the Lord as we charismatics do? Isn't the whole parish set-up just an example of a dead institution that is carried forward only by its own inertia?

The Catholic parish, whether it is spiritually renewed or not, remains a place where any Catholic, if he so desires, can still have contact with Christianity at least on the level of culture. It is perhaps the last great institution in Western culture that maintains a sense of "Christendom" for the Catholic. One can still go there and associate with persons who share Christian values. One's children can go to school with other children whose parents are making some effort to raise them decently. One can work together with others in conducting Christian social events, in working for the poor, in trying to learn about Christian responses to current issues. This happens in addition to the parish's spiritual function of ministering the sacraments and holding up the truths of the faith on a regular basis in the liturgy and through educational means. Yes, it would be wonderful if all parishes gave spiritual issues higher priority. But we must recognize that they are performing a great work for the Lord when, in addition to their sacred ministry, they maintain themselves as places where Catholics can gather, even when such gatherings are mainly for cultural purposes.

Development of Parish Prayer Groups

Prayer groups start in many different ways. Most of the first groups began as a result of contact with denominational Pentecostals or with some of the early university-based groups at Duquesne, Notre Dame, the University of Michigan and other places. As time passed, groups began to spring up in a variety of ways. Some began after a charismatic conference, when those who were filled with the Spirit at the conference brought the experience back to their city or town. Others developed when a person who was attending an existing meeting left it and started his own group. Still others started when a large, city-wide prayer group split up into smaller groups in each parish. Some were started by the Spirit directly with little or no mediation on the part of an already existing group.

Whatever may have served as the initial impulse, most groups have eventually moved to set themselves up as their parish's charismatic prayer group.

This has happened as a natural consequence of the fact that Catholics see their spiritual lives in terms of life in the parish setting. In addition, it has been encouraged by the church, for several reasons. First, it recognizes the need for spiritual renewal in our time and, having discerned the potential in charismatic life for personal and communal spiritual renewal, it desires to make it its own through fostering it in parishes. Of course, the church has also drawn the charismatic renewal to itself by giving it links on the diocesan, national and international level, but in this chapter we are focusing on the parish. In addition, it wants to foster the work of the Spirit in whatever ways he is moving in the lives of Catholics, and makes a place for the charismatic parish-centered experience as a service to the faithful. Also, it sees the need for protecting and safeguarding what God is doing in the lives of Catholic charismatics, and so directs them to the parish where sound and prudent guidance can be provided.

The parochial setting strengthens prayer-group members by enabling them to integrate their enriched charismatic experience of the Spirit into the traditional aspects of Catholic life and spirituality. This is especially true when the pastor or one of his assistants is either charismatic or favorably disposed to the renewal. Charismatic Masses, penance services, healing services, etc., provide opportunities for a deepened awareness of the presence of the Spirit in sacramental life. Prayer-group members also grow in their appreciation of Catholic spirituality. They begin to have a greater sense of being part of the overall mission of the parish. Often they become more involved in various noncharismatic areas of parish ministry.

However, difficulties eventually begin to surface as charismatic parishioners continue their efforts to combine their experience with parish life. Two basic problems normally surface. The first is resentment and negative feeling on the part of the rest of the parish. The prayer group naturally wants to share its new-found life in the Spirit with others in the parish, and members long for the time when the whole parish will be Spirit-filled. Their longing is never shared by most parishioners, who begin to become irritated by the "pushy charismatics," who insist that their way of being Christian is so superior. This development causes the group to become somewhat isolated from the rest of the parish.

The other common problem is the conflict of loyalties that develops within the prayer group between being involved with one another and being good parishioners. If the group is truly led by the Spirit in prophecy, discernment and counsel, the Lord is able gradually to draw participants into greater unity with one another. They begin to spend increasing amounts of time and energy helping one another to grow in Christ, especially with regard to their character

formation, sexuality, family lives and societal experience—
the "new problems" mentioned by the *Decree on the Laity*.

The group focuses inward, which further isolates it from
the rest of the parish. Parish pastors, who have the good of
the whole parish as their responsibility, grow concerned
that the group sustain its loyalty to the parish and not
develop into a group that exists only for its own sake. They
call on participants to refocus their spiritual lives within the
parish and to avoid doing things which might cause them to
become elitist or divisive. In most cases, prayer groups
follow the lead of their priests and sacrifice greater unity
among themselves for the sake of parish unity.

As these external difficulties gradually surface, the group
also begins to experience internal pressures. After their initial period of enthusiasm dies down, they must face the
problems that every prayer group encounters, such as lack
of organization, vision and leadership, competition between
leaders, some men being too timid and some women being
too aggressive, lack of theological formation, and spiritual
immaturity. Also, addressing the new problems becomes a
difficult burden to carry, and the participants start to recoil
from this task.

If the conflicts and difficulties just described are not
resolved, the parish prayer group loses its forward momentum. Some groups grow weak and eventually dissolve.
Others lower their sights and become pious devotional groups
within the parish. Some members are embittered against the
parish and form their own groups totally outside the parish
structures. In rare cases, where the group is led by a strong
priest or layperson, these problems are overcome and the
group is able to maintain its unity in the Spirit while remain-
ing loyal to the parish.

Not all prayer groups in the parishes have to confront the
problems we have been discussing. Some groups exist in
parishes where loyalty to the parish is so strong that the
issue of conflict of loyalties never arises. Some are com-
posed of persons who do not experience problems in their
personal lives in the way that most Christians do in contemporary society. This is often the case in conservative Catholic parishes that have effectively countered the secularizing

pressures of modern life. Still other groups have the tact and maturity to avoid alienating outsiders. But such situations are exceptions. The life of the normal parish prayer group tends to unfold in the problematic way outlined above.

Nonparish Groups

Groups which are not led in the direction of parish-centeredness usually have a history that is substantially different from that of parish groups. These groups develop in one of two directions, depending on whether or not the leadership and members of the group have a real love for the church. Augustine says, "A man possesses the Holy Spirit in the measure in which he loves the Church" (quoted in *Decree on the Training of Priests*, 9).

Those who do not love the church do not believe they have a duty to interact positively with the parish. They feel that in their group Christianity is really being lived correctly; they view institutional Catholic life as peripheral to being an authentic Christian. They put themselves outside the pastoral guidance and ministry of the parish, except perhaps for sacramental ministry. Gradually this results in the emergence of the belief that their group and groups like it are the *real* church, and that all other manifestations of Christianity ought to be judged in terms of their experience of the Lord. Groups which take this path are out of the Spirit and constitute a grave aberration from God's plan for our time. Their mistakes have led many in the church to become suspicious of the charismatic experience and have greatly hindered the work of the Spirit.

Some groups love the church but are called by the Lord along extra-parochial lines. Often these groups made initial attempts to fit into the parish setting, but either the parish rejected the group or was unable to give it the kind of direction and ministry it desired. For example, members of a typical group might have told their pastors excitedly about the baptism in the Spirit and suggested that it was for the whole parish. They probably received a skeptical response, although the priests would be polite and perhaps somewhat encouraging. Usually, nothing happened. Meanwhile, the group would move forward powerfully in the Spirit. People would overcome sins they had been fighting for years. Healings would occur. The Lord would bring many people to repentance and salvation. The corrupting influence of modern society would be lessened.

As time would pass, the group would see that much of its work could have not taken place in a normal parish setting. Though they might not feel quite right about this in terms of their preconciliar vision of the role of the laity, they could not deny the evident good results which accompanied their efforts outside the parish. Eventually they would see that it was the intent of the Spirit to have them function in a nonparish-centered way so that he could minister to their lives in a way that was not possible within parish pastoral structures.

At the same time, however, the Lord would make it very clear to the group that it must not abandon parishes. On the contrary, participants would sense an increasing obligation to their respective parishes and to the church as a whole. They would begin to look for ways to aid the parish in its ongoing life, though not necessarily along charismatic lines.

The difficulties encountered by these groups, other than the normal prayer-group problems with immaturity, leadership infighting, etc., usually involve keeping up positive and fruitful relationships with the clergy and with other parishioners. Their system for taking care of one another, though it is usually sound from the conciliar point of view, is easily misunderstood by outsiders, who tend to challenge the group's competency and authority to deal with the problems it addresses. Many groups are not able to withstand the pressure put on them in this regard. Such groups stop functioning, and their members either abandon charismatic life or seek out some kind of parish-centered group.

However, hundreds of nonparish groups have survived and are thriving today. About one hundred of them are called "covenant communities." These are groups which have solemnly committed themselves to share their whole lives in Christ with one another in order to create a level of Christian life that is reflective of New Testament Christianity.

There are also many successful nonparish prayer groups which are not covenant communities, where personal and corporate life produces much good fruit. It remains to be seen how the Lord will use nonparish groups to help renew parishes.

The Present Situation

The charismatic experience has not reached its full potential in the parish setting. This is because, on the one hand, those responsible for parish prayer groups have not yet grasped the extent of the council's enriched vision for lay participation in parish ministry. On the other hand, those in successful nonparish groups have not yet found a way to engage in fruitful dialogue with their parishes, especially with regard to overcoming the new problems. I would now like to offer some suggestions to charismatics on working through these difficulties, so that the parish can fully benefit from the Lord's work in the renewal.

Let us first consider the situation of nonparish groups. The histories of these groups normally display five sources of difficulty with local parishes. The first is weakness in charity on both sides. Noncharismatic parish priests and parishioners often fall short in treating charismatics with basic Christian charity. This is especially true with regard to their speech. However, prayer groups often fail in this same regard, not only with respect to speech, but through impatience and arrogance. Both groups must have as their first goal the increase of charity. If this goal is kept in view, most other difficulties will be relatively easy to deal with.

Second, there are often poor lines of communication between the two parties. Charismatics must take the initiative in this area. They cannot expect pastors or other parishioners to chase after them so as to get on better terms. Parishes and priests have more than enough to think about. It would be arrogant for prayer groups to wait for the parish to come to them.

Third, this is a difficult time for the church, especially in terms of the role of laypersons and the emergence of new lay movements and structures within the church. Since the council, many unresolved issues have surfaced in this regard. Patient thought and work on the part of clergy, theologians and participants is needed so that the present confusion can be cleared up in a way that does not quench the Holy Spirit as he moves in new and richer ways among the laity.

Fourth, misunderstanding often comes from an inability to understand the dynamic and evolving nature of the charismatic movement. Mistakes made yesterday may be corrected today. This often happens in the case of my own group, which is nonparish-centered. I sometimes hear criticism that is based on what someone said 8 or 10 years ago. Usually the person is not even part of the group anymore. The mistake has long since been corrected, but it is seen by outsiders as typical of what we do. The whole charismatic renewal is in the formative stages of its development and probably will be for some time to come. With this awareness, problem situations can be seen in a different (and better) light.

On the other hand, we in the renewal must understand that, as Catholic author Gene Geissler has said, "This thing is almost impossible to understand from the outside." His statement is particularly true with regard to the many aspects of the movement that are still evolving.

Also, we must realize that the good news which is so evident to those inside the renewal is not as newsworthy as bad news in the minds of outsiders.

Fifth, some of the difficulty comes from the Lord himself, who uses the wider church to test the faithfulness of the renewal. The church has often functioned in this way for religious renewals in the past. This is not, of course, a criticism of the church, but simply a statement of spiritual fact which is obvious to anyone who has studied church history.

Having considered some general sources of difficulty, let us now discuss specific objections raised about nonparish-centered groups.

*   *   *

Objection One: The leaders of such groups usurp authority which properly resides in the church through her bishops and priests.

Although there are failings in individual cases (remember that we are not talking about groups who disdain the parish, but about those who love their parish), the teaching and practice of such groups largely avoid what is properly the clerical domain. They do not say their own Masses, hear confessions or teach and preach on Catholic doctrine in the name of the church, except in the sense that any Christian has the right to talk about the truth. The areas in which they do exercise leadership are almost always within the domain of lay ministry as it is defined in the *Decree on the Laity.* If there were more positive communication between both sides, this first objection would be much less common.

Objection Two: Such groups weaken parishes by drawing them away from parish life.

The opposite is usually true. Many, if not most of the members of these groups were previously either not Christian at all or were minimal Catholics who were not involved in parish life to begin with. Even those who were solid Catholics beforehand usually join to maintain their dedication to the Lord. If these persons had not joined, many might have fallen away from dedicated Christianity because of the lack of support in most parish situations. When one adds to these arguments the fact that support of one's parish is usually encouraged in the prayer group, the net result is that participation in parish life is normally increased. If these groups did not exist, some members would probably invest themselves more in their parish, but many would be less involved or not involved at all.

Objection Three: These groups should not function outside the authority of the pastor, but ought to submit themselves to priests and become subgroups within the parishes.

This approach, which has been tried in several places, causes several difficulties. First, if the group is successful, it could easily become a source of division within the parish. The members of a typical nonparish group experience a high degree of unity and solidarity. They often tend to accomplish different tasks with greater success and efficiency than normal parish groups. The priest who becomes involved with the group would become endeared to it (and it would become endeared to him) as a result of the closeness and richness of its life. This situation can cause other parishioners to feel left out, neglected by the priest, resentful because of the group's success, etc.

Another aspect of nonparish groups that argues against them being parish-contained is that they usually deal in a substantial way with the new problems, and this calls for a significant investment of time and effort. If a pastor were to lead such a group effectively, he would have much less time for his other duties. Monopolizing a priest's time would only increase the possibilities of division.

Objection Four: Is not the ecumenical nature of some of these groups dangerous to the Catholic faith of those members who are Catholic?

In answer to this question, which is certainly valid in the case of those groups which do not cultivate a love for the parish, one must look at the fruit of grass-roots ecumenical dialogue in the groups we are discussing. There are no statistics on the matter as yet. In my experience (I have substantial contact with dozens of these groups), ecumenical groups actually have a positive effect on the Catholicism of their members. Many who had left the church or who were on their way out are brought back because the group offers them a way of being Catholic that is an alternative to their previously unsatisfying membership in the church. Many who are loyal Catholics experience an enriched and more hopeful Catholicism. Also, many others join the Catholic Church through these groups, not because they are proselytized, but because they see at close range the rich-ness of the church in the daily lives of Catholic participants.

What should these groups do now and in the future? They should resolve to strive for an increase of charity toward their brothers and sisters in Christ in their parishes. They should prudently work to open better lines of commu-nication with those in pastoral authority in their parishes and dioceses. They should take steps to gain more sound theological training, especially if they are leaders. Many difficulties in the area we are considering are theological. Better training can enable more successful dialogue to take place. They should seek clergy and make efforts to befriend them. This is better than viewing them as persons who "just do not understand," who need to "get with it," and so on.

It is not yet clear what the Lord's long-range plans are for nonparish-centered groups. Should they seek official church status of some sort, as some have already done? Should they eventually fade into existing parish structures? Should they remain as they are now; voluntary associations of laypersons and clergy?* Does the Lord have some other plan? We will have to wait on his word spoken in our hearts and through the church for the answers to these questions.

The Situation of Parish Groups

Some parish groups are able to sustain themselves and successfully live the Spirit-filled life, but most last for a time and then dissolve or lose their vision. Assuming they can handle normal prayer-group difficulties such as immaturity, leadership infighting, etc., I believe that these groups fail for two basic reasons: lack of support from the clergy and

---

*Many of these groups, though they are not contained within the parish structure, are strongly united to the institutional church on the diocesan and/or national level. Their life seems to be developing along the lines of the broader Catholic tradition of diocesan and universal movements, associations, etc. Such movements are given specific en-couragement in the *Decree on the Laity* (18–22).

failure to address successfully the new problems of today's society. The first obstacle can be overcome if priests show more openness to the sections of the council documents which point to the fostering of charisms in lay life. One key section was quoted at the beginning of the chapter. In another section, the church explicitly instructs priests to foster the charisms: "They (priests) must discover with faith, recognize with joy, and foster with diligence the many and varied charismatic gifts of the laity" (*Decree on Priestly Ministry*, 9). Pope John Paul II, in his 1981 address to worldwide leaders of the renewal, made a similar point when he taught that "priests must adopt a welcoming attitude toward charismatics."

With regard to overcoming the new problems of today, I would like to offer a few suggestions which may help move things forward. These suggestions are based on my observations over the last 16 years of how parish and nonparish groups have attempted to cope with these problems.

Suggestion One: Decide to confront the new problems.

There are several reasons why the new problems are not addressed effectively in most parish prayer groups. First, most persons who seek the baptism in the Spirit simply do not want to deal with them. I know that I didn't. They just desire something more than their prior Christian life seemed to offer. But in the course of life in the Spirit, the Lord usually leads participants to the threshold of this area. Many turn back at this point because they sense, often unconsciously, that such a path is a very difficult one to embark upon.

Another reason why groups recoil from addressing the new problems is that participants instinctively sense that the pastoral structure of the parish is not set up to deal with them. Trying to be good parishioners, they back off and leave ministry in this area to priests, who try to deal with them in the confessional, in counselling sessions, or by directing persons to professional counsellors.

A third reason for recoiling from this area is that clergymen who are associated with the prayer groups see such ministry as mainly the domain of the priest. Addressing such difficulties, they feel, involves speaking with spiritual authority, which they see as the task of priestly "sacred ministry." They believe that such practices as in-depth marriage counselling, instruction on how to overcome sexual sins, giving *de-facto* spiritual direction, and comprehensive training in Christian behavior are not only dangerous ministries for laypersons to take on, but are ministries of the spiritual and not of the secular or temporal order, which is where most lay ministry should be taking place.

Fourth, some Catholics, both lay and clergy, simply do not understand how desperate a need there is for ministry in this area. Some are living in the past and think that people's problems are no worse than they used to be. Others are so confused by the swirl of change that has engulfed the church and the world in the past 20 years that they are unable to think clearly anymore about the issues we are discussing.

The motives for recoiling from the new problems in parish prayer groups are understandable. Participants are correct in sensing that the area is a difficult one to become involved in. The perception that parishes are not set up to deal with these problems is also correct. Priests are right in pointing out that their ministry in the spiritual order must be respected. One cannot fault some others for failing to realize the difficulty of the present situation. We are all only beginning to wake up to this reality.

But such persons fail to recognize three things. First, one cannot renew the church of today without addressing these problems. It is no accident that the Lord leads charismatic groups in the direction of solving them. If they are left untended, the group will have no personal, family and societal foundations to stand on as it tries to do all the other things the Lord wants it to do. The same thing is true with any Christian grouping. If people's personal and environmental lives are in disarray, they will never succeed in implementing programs for renewal, no matter how well they are organized and led.

Second, parishes cannot avoid problems just because they

are not currently set up to minister to them. Parishes that take this course of least resistance abrogate their duty to care for those in need. If they don't help out, who will? Parishes must be willing to experiment with new structures until they find ones which will solve the problems.

Third, the *Decree on the Laity* calls on laypersons to address such issues. (See sections 9, 10, 11.) The church understands that problems in keeping one's family from collapsing, building a social setting which protects one's children from the neopagan aspects of our culture, personal problems such as gross sexual immorality, drug abuse, alcohol abuse, etc.—all of which are common among Catholics— cannot be dealt with simply by hearing confessions, giving good advice, having meaningful liturgies, putting on renewal retreats, etc. In the decree, the church teaches that major pastoral effort by clergy and laity in cooperation with one another is needed.

Suggestion Two: Choose as leaders persons with the capacity to lead others in solving the new problems.

Often prayer groups are started by persons who have good organizational skills or who have natural charisma. Such persons do not necessarily have the gifts and maturity needed to guide a group through the difficult areas we are discussing. The priest associated with the group, along with the mature members of the group, must be able to discern prayerfully who can serve as leader(s). Those who are called by the Lord must not be timid or unwilling to make the sacrifices necessary in the role they are asked to play.

Suggestion Three: Develop an initiation system and an ongoing teaching and pastoral function that counters the new problems.

This is the most complex and difficult part of the task of dealing with these problems. Prayer groups can make progress by seeking out those groups, whether parish or nonparish, which are already successful in pastoring persons in this way. They can read the literature on these subjects, go personally to the groups for advice, and even establish ongoing relationships with them.

Suggestion Four: Go forward with the priest. Don't go forward without him.

We have several times made the point that involvement of the clergy in parish groups is important to their success. It becomes crucial if the group enters the path of confronting the new problems. Without his involvement at this point, the possibilities for misunderstanding and confusion become so great as to make it inadvisable to go ahead without his support and, if possible, active involvement. Also, the spiritual authority which is his because of his ordination and his pastoral and theological expertise will be an invaluable asset to the group.

In this chapter, we have examined the interface between the charismatic experience and parish life. Unlike what has been done in the other chapters, our discussion has not focused on the enrichments of faith produced by charismatic life, though there are many. Rather, because the renewal has not yet ministered to the parishes in the way that many had hoped it would, we have centered our discussion on the difficulties that exist in the area and have offered some suggestions as to how to overcome some of these difficulties. In the case of nonparish groups, we have suggested greater charity and better lines of communication, along with an openness to what the Lord may say in the future. With regard to parish groups, we have suggested that the Lord's work can be helped if priests take a more positive attitude toward parish groups and if the groups decide to face the new problems in a prudent way, seeking, among other things, to learn from the groups that have already dealt with new problems successfully.

There has been an enormous amount of thought and discussion in the renewal with regard to the issues brought up in this chapter. It is my hope that what has been said will shed further light in the area.

Let me end by making a final suggestion. Charismatics who are really serious about parish renewal must study the *Decree on the Apostolate of Lay People*. The implementation of this decree is crucial to the future of the church, and we charismatics, with our love for the church and experience in efforts at renewal, are in an ideal position to incorporate its vision into our lives.

CHAPTER 5:

Catholic Evangelism

Catholic evangelism, in so far as it involves directly bringing people to accept Christ and his gospel, has traditionally been the task of clergy and religious. Most missionary work was done by priests, nuns and brothers. In the parish setting, the priest was usually the person who brought the convert into the church and taught him or her the basics of Catholic doctrine and life.

Since the council, which teaches that "each disciple of Christ has the obligation of spreading the gospel to the best of his/her ability" (*Constitution on the Church*, 17), the church has with increasing insistence called on all Catholics to participate actively in a ministry of evangelism. However, although this call of the Lord through the church has been proclaimed for almost 20 years, the spirit of evangelism is not yet fully alive at the grass-roots level.

There are several reasons for this. First, the development of an evangelistic consciousness in the minds of Catholics involves enormous changes in the way we view our Catholic life. Our habitual perspective has been one which emphasized living a life according to catechism-taught truths of faith and morals, being ministered to in the parish by the sacraments, and, for the educated, knowing the rational arguments in favor of Catholic Christianity. We left preaching to the priests.

Second, witnessing to the gospel is inextricably bound up with knowing what the gospel is, i.e., knowing the scriptures. Those Christian denominations which seem to be most successful today at the level of grass-roots evangelism rely heavily on the New Testament in their spiritual lives. Catholics are only beginning to understand how valuable knowing the words of scripture can be, not only in the area of witnessing, but in every area of the Christian life.

A third reason for the weakness of evangelistic witness on the part of the faithful is that Catholics themselves need to be evangelized before they can tell others about the Lord, as has been pointed out by almost every leader in the church since the council. The statement is often made that Catholics have been sacramentalized but not evangelized. We have been led by the church through sacramental rituals and have been taught the meaning of these rituals, but we have not been adequately taught about the centrality of having a personal relationship with Christ in our lives. One might add that, for the past 20 years, Catholics have also been psychologized in addition to being sacramentalized, but we still have not yet been adequately evangelized. By this I mean that the church has done a lot lately to sort out for the faithful the psychological dimension of belief, especially with regard to guilt and love. While this has been helpful, the basic issue of personal commitment to Christ has yet to be addressed effectively.

The charismatic renewal is perhaps the only movement in the church that has dealt with the above three problems successfully. With regard to changing one's perspective, the baptism in the Spirit produces in a person's heart an immediate desire to share the gospel with others, even though he or she might not have the expert training of clergy or religious. The renewal is also a back-to-the-Bible movement. Through it, we come to see our whole Christian lives more as a living out of the words of scripture. Included in our more scripturally oriented vision of Catholic life is the biblical call to witness to Christ. With respect to the need for evangelizing Catholics, the charismatic renewal, along with movements such as the *Cursillo, Focolare, Opus Dei* and others, calls for a deeper conversion to Christ as part of becoming active in the movement.

A recent statement of the National Diocesan Liaisons Committee for the Charismatic Renewal demonstrates the great impact the renewal has had on the witness lives of laypersons. (The information that follows was taken from the newsletter of the National Service Committee, November, 1982.)

> "—The vast majority of people involved in organized evangelization efforts in the parishes have a background in the Charismatic Renewal.
> —At an evangelization conference in the fall of 1981, some 70% of the participants were active in charismatic prayer groups.
> —The Life in the Spirit Seminars parallel very closely the new rite of Christian Initiation of Adults (RCIA). Many parishes have effectively used the LSS as part of the Christian Initiation process.
> —Where the Catholic Church is becoming involved in radio and TV broadcasting, the people in the Charismatic Renewal are particularly active.
> —The majority of Bible-study group leaders come from the Charismatic Renewal."

Also, many lessons learned by charismatics in their evangelistic efforts are applicable to the situation of the broader church. The same committee made the following statement:

> "Through the renewal, the Spirit has taught that:
> —Evangelism should normally be accompanied by healings.
> —The goal of evangelization should be to become incorporated into a Jesus Community and to continue an ever deepening conversion to holiness.

—Witness from a faith community becomes a key
    evangelistic method.
—Prayer—especially praise—and music have pow-
    ers that have not yet been fully employed for
    evangelization.
—Anointed preaching must be included as a power
    resource for effective evangelization.
—Bishops who rely on the power of the Spirit are
    needed to feed their flocks."

Having acknowledged that the charismatic experience leads
to the enrichment of one's faith in the area of evangelism,
we might ask, what is the essence of this enrichment? What
key insight about living a life which witnesses to the gospel
has the Lord taught us in the renewal?

Although we have learned that preaching, healing, intercession, etc., are valuable assets in sharing the gospel, the
main way the Lord enriches evangelism among charismatics
is by reorienting their personal day-to-day relationships more
toward witnessing. The more spectacular aspects of charismatic evangelism are helpful, but we have learned that the
main work of bringing others to Christ is performed by
individuals in person-to-person relationships with those
whom the Lord brings into their lives.

Thus, the most important task we face, as we work to
bring the faithful to the point where they are effective
witnesses, is to give each layperson an understanding of
the life of witnessing that enables him to take action in
the area. If we as Catholics can cultivate among ourselves
an understanding of how to witness in our daily lives, the
main hindrances to witnessing at the grass-roots level will
have been overcome.

Cultivating an Apostolic Consciousness

All of us can be successful in witnessing to the gospel in
our daily lives if we cultivate an apostolic consciousness.

If we are able to develop a habitual perspective toward
our lives which constantly looks for and notices opportuni-

ties for witnessing to Christ, we will soon see that the Lord provides us with many opportunities every day for witnessing to his saving love. The following are 14 basic guidelines which have been successfully applied by many of us in the renewal in our efforts to become more effective witnesses.*

Sustain the Zeal of the First Hour

When we first accept the Lord and his Spirit, we are usually on fire with a zeal to share with others the pearl of great price which we have just uncovered. For many, this first fervor is a catalyst which leads to successful evangelism. But, when the fervor wears off, so does our zeal for souls. Later on, we look back on our evangelistic successes of the initial phase of life in the Spirit and wonder what it was that made our efforts so fruitful. Some explain it in terms of having a special grace which seemed to fade after a while. Others note that their successes were with persons they knew, and that, once these persons had been witnessed to, they had no more opportunities to witness to Christ. Still others explain that, at first, all they did was go around witnessing, and that their effectiveness decreased as they began to pay attention to other aspects of following Christ.

All these explanations have some merit to them. But, as I have observed the lives of some friends who continue to be effective in bringing others to Christ long after the initial zeal has worn off, I have noticed that they do not seem to be hindered by the situations mentioned above. One reason for this is that they possess a zeal which is similar to the zeal we all have in "the first hour." The difference between their zeal and the typically experienced first fervor is that they make deliberate efforts to maintain their zeal. Thus, they habitually possess a catalyst which triggers evangelistic activity.

We need to attach greater value to the zeal manifested when we first accepted the Lord. We need to understand

*Some of what will follow has been drawn from the literature of the *Cursillo.*

that it is used by him to give us the energy and heart to invest ourselves in witnessing. We need to realize that, by cultivating this zeal in our spiritual lives, we can sustain it and make it a normal part of our spiritual perspective.

Maintain Forward Momentum

Often we talk about guarding against backsliding in our life in the Spirit. The point is made that if we are not going forward in Christ, then we are losing ground. If we do not gather with Christ, then we will scatter.

The same can be said about our life of witness. If we do not cultivate a sacrificial spirit with regard to evangelism, being willing to take on increased burdens for the Lord if he sends them, we will tend to drift in the other direction. We need regularly to check ourselves in this matter by asking how much time and energy we have been spending in witnessing to the Lord, how conscious we are of the possibilities for evangelism in our daily lives, and when the last time was that we made a special sacrifice for the sake of someone's conversion to the Lord.

Work Within the Range of the Possible:
Leave the Impossible to the Lord

Paul tells us in his letter to the Romans, ". . . think with sober judgment, each according to the measure of faith which God has assigned him" (Rom. 12:3). Not all of us are able to stand up and preach the gospel at a public meeting. Some may be good at street evangelism; others may not. Some may be able to talk to students about the Lord; others are skilled at sharing with businessmen or homemakers. We need to understand our skills and abilities in witnessing and use them when occasions present themselves. We should not try to evangelize in a way that is beyond or outside our capabilities. I used to try to talk to persons on the street, but never met with any success. A friend who knew better how to share in this way was quite successful. On the other hand, I was much more effective in sharing with students than he was. Eventually I confined myself to work with students, and he focused mainly on street witnessing.

As we work within the range of our abilities, even though the range may be narrow, we will be blessed by the Lord. As we are successful with the talents he gives us, he will increase our possibilities and give us new talents which enable us to do more for him.

Some situations we may confront may involve "impossible" cases. These should be offered in intercessory prayer to the Lord, with whom all things are possible.

Cultivate an Authentic Spirituality

If we attempt to witness to others while not living authentically Christian lives ourselves, there is a good chance that they will see through our words and dismiss us as hypocrites. This not only causes them to reject the gospel we preach now, but makes them less open to it when others share with them in the future.

There are several common tendencies in the witnessing of some that we should be especially careful to avoid. The first, which is particularly a danger among Catholics, is minimalism. We cannot convince others to commit their whole lives to Christ when we ourselves actually practice the faith in a minimal way that consists only of obeying the rules. We must have at least as deep a commitment to the Lord as we are suggesting to them. We must also avoid sounding like elitists who have all the answers. We may, in fact, have a lot of answers that our hearers need to accept, but a holier-than-thou attitude will usually block their ears from hearing them. Most important, we must avoid the tendency to Phariseeism, by which I mean defining conversion to the Lord in terms of accepting rules and regulations that we happen to be skilled in applying. This tendency, which we sometimes unconsciously adopt, blocks the way to Christ for many, and even puts us outside the Lord's kingdom, as was the case with the Pharisees of Jesus' time.

On the positive side, our spirituality must first be joyful.

The Lord has done so much for us that we should rejoice always in our hearts. This joy must be communicated to those we are witnessing to, especially in our day, when life seems particularly distressing and lacking in joy. We must also be natural and avoid coming across as stiff and formal, as though we were delivering some kind of set formula to our hearers. Men should be manly and aggressive; women should be feminine and not hard or pushy. Finally, all of us, men and women alike, must have a bold and courageous attitude as we share, not a timid, apologetic demeanor. If we do not share with strength and confidence, we will be much less convincing to those we witness to.

Study Scripture

We have already mentioned this aspect of developing a successful spirituality of evangelism. There is no substitute for knowing scripture when we share the gospel. Not only does the Bible say more clearly than any other book what needs to be communicated, but the words of scripture carry with them spiritual power that would not be there otherwise. I have several times tried to explain something about God's ways in my own terms and failed, but then quoted the Bible on the matter and turned the whole situation around.

In the renewal, we have an ideal environment for growing in our knowledge of scripture. We need more and more to use the knowledge we have gained in our witness lives. We may make some mistakes at first because of an overly simplistic understanding of the Bible, but, as we persevere in utilizing it, we will find that it is a powerful help in evangelism.

Sacramental Life

I mentioned above that the Eucharist is the source and summit of all evangelization. An effective witness-life must be founded on regular reception of Communion. In addition to giving us the vitality to evangelize and giving those we witness to an ultimate goal to arrive at in their conversion, the Eucharist can be the direct source of providential evangelistic encounters. As I write this book, I can recall four occasions in the past six months when, after receiving Communion, I met someone I was able to witness to as I left church. I believe that, as we open our spiritual eyes to such providential occurrences, they will happen in our lives in a regular way.

The other sacraments are also supportive of our witness life.

Bring Plans and Ideas into the Concrete

St. James tells us that we must not "be just hearers but also doers of the word" (James 1:22). If an opportunity presents itself, we must not simply think about how we might respond. We must actually do something. Often we hear someone talk about ways to witness and agree in our hearts that the person is right and decide to implement the teaching. But, when the time to act arrives, we rationalize our way out of doing what we had previously decided was right to do. Too many of us are good armchair witnesses who never act on what we believe.

We sometimes have good reasons for hesitating when evangelistic opportunities come our way. Will they misunderstand us? Will we seem too pushy? Will they think we are crazy?

But there is an even better reason not to hesitate. If we don't tell them about the Lord, who will? This may be a key moment in their lives that the Lord has been preparing them for. It may be their last chance to come to know him. Fortified by these arguments, we must take risks, even if they don't always seem to work out the way we had hoped. As people who have an active witness-life will testify, even our apparent failures in witnessing are used by the Lord in ways that might not be evident for years.

Use the Obstacles the Lord Sends Us

Scripture tells us, "Rejoice in this when you suffer various trials, so that the genuineness of your faith, tested by fire, may redound to the glory of Jesus Christ" (1 Pt. 6: 7). A life of active evangelizing is usually full of trials, obstacles and failures. The Lord uses these things to reveal to us our hidden weaknesses and to train us in heroism. We need to respond to these difficulties in a positive way and discern what it is the Lord is trying to accomplish. He led us into witnessing. If we seem to fail, it is because he is doing something with us to make us stronger in him and better able in the future to do his work.

Discouragement at the obstacles in our way is usually the main cause of losing our initial zeal. By simply changing our attitude toward these obstacles we will accomplish a great deal in our efforts to sustain that zeal.

Use Opportunities That Present Themselves

We should look at all areas of our lives and see how they can be converted into occasions for witness. Everything we do—whether on the job, at home, in the parish, in social organizations, etc.—should be examined. When I began to think in this way, I was amazed at how many more opportunities for witnessing I discovered in my life. As we employ this guideline, we must not develop a way of relating that becomes overly preachy.

Always Discern the Body

The recommendations of the diocesan liaisons listed earlier in the chapter state that "witness from a faith community becomes a key evangelistic method." We must be careful in our witness-lives to avoid the tendency to become spiritual Lone Rangers. Christ set up his body in such a way that the parts need one another, and our apostolate of evangelism must be conducted with this truth in mind. Most of us will experience more success if we work as part of a group that evangelizes. Those who have worked on evangelistic retreats such as *Cursillos* or on Life in the Spirit Seminar teams can attest to this fact. What they could never have done as individuals is accomplished with great effectiveness when done as a unified team.

Some who have special gifts experience great success as witnesses through their own individual efforts. But these persons also must "discern the body" in their work. They need a faith community to which they can lead those they share with. Connectedness with other Christians can be a protection for these individuals so that they do not become proud as a result of their successes and drift away from God's plan for their lives, leading others away with them.

Cultivate a Victorious Spirit

Paul tells us in his letter to the Romans (Rom. 8:31), "If God is for us, then who is against us?" As we share with others about the Lord, we must impart to them a sense of hope and enthusiasm. Thus, we need first to make this victorious, hopeful spirit a habitual part of our spiritual perspective. The Christian road, narrow and difficult as it is, can seem at times to be burdensome. This is especially the case during times of spiritual testing or dryness. However, on a more basic level, the gospel life is always one which should stir up within us a sense of triumph and optimism. Jesus has died and is risen. He has overcome death, sin and the devil. He has a place prepared for us with him in eternity. This victorious optimism should always accompany our times of witnessing to the gospel. If we don't feel spiritually victorious as we prepare to share with someone, we should turn to the Lord, meditating on the truths just mentioned and asking him to stir up these sentiments in our hearts.

Be All Things to All so That Some May Be Saved

Christ calls us to love all persons, but he also wants us to love them intelligently. We need to understand what is in each person's heart, as our Lord did, and then consider how the gospel might best be communicated to him. With some, we may offer tracts. We might ask others on a retreat. We might share with one person immediately after meeting him. We might not speak to another until we know him well. We might never share the gospel with some, but simply witness to Christ through our example. We might try to get another person to meet one of our friends if we feel he will respond better to him, and so on. As we strive to cultivate an apostolic consciousness, we will find it necessary to do a lot of hard thinking and planning, so that we can, in love, make the decision that is best for those whom the Lord leads to us.

Having regular contact with others who try to live active evangelistic lives is especially helpful in applying this last rule of thumb. We normally do not have enough ability as individuals to sort out all the issues involved in loving all persons intelligently. Still, if we are able to share with others who are working on the same types of problems, as happens, for example, in the group reunions of the *Cursillo*, we will greatly increase our chances of making decisions that are the most loving for those we are witnessing to.

Go to God About Men Before You Go to Men About God

This slogan, taken from the *Cursillo* literature, expresses in an easy-to-remember way a key principle of all personal evangelism. In sharing the gospel, we are doing something which is of absolute importance to the Lord. More than anything else he wants people to believe in him so that they can experience eternal union with him in heaven. Therefore, he wants to lead and guide us in our efforts and asks us to go to him in prayer to find out just how we should proceed.

When we "go to God about men" we should pray in two ways. First, we should intercede for the person we are planning to share with and make sacrifices for the sake of his or her conversion. Typical sacrifices might be fasting or keeping vigil. Second, we should ask the Lord for specific guidance how to proceed. Is now the right time to talk to him or her? Should I bring another person along? Should I preach from scripture? Should I use other terms? Not only do we need to think about how to love people, but we need also to know the Lord's supernatural plan for that person.

Let the Spirit Blow Where He Wills

Those who are most successful in personal evangelism always leave room for the Lord to move providentially in the lives of those they are witnessing to. They learn to work around what God is doing. They look for clues when God providentially intervenes in someone's life so that they can see more clearly how he wants to move. They adjust their efforts so as to fit in better with the Lord's design.

I was sharing several years ago with a young man who was seeking a fuller life in Christ. At the time, he held many mistaken views with regard to scripture and Catholic doctrine, and these views were the main spiritual obstacle to his progress. At first, I thought it would take a long time for him to sort out his erroneous positions, and estimated that many long conversations would be required before he got his thinking straightened out. But then he began to go to confession to an excellent priest-confessor. Within a few weeks, his ideas were corrected and the Spirit was able to move powerfully with him. The Lord had providentially accomplished a task which, according to my timetable, would have taken much longer. It also helped me understand that the Lord wanted to work sacramentally with the young man, strengthening his faith as he participated more in the sacraments. So, I began to encourage him more to go to confession and Communion, rather than trying to lead him out of theological difficulties through long discussions.

*   *   *

In this chapter, we have considered how the charismatic renewal has enriched Catholic evangelism in America and have listed some guidelines for personal evangelism which have been effective in the lives of many charismatics. The potential among rank-and-file Catholics for winning persons to Christ is enormous; in the charismatic renewal, we have only seen the beginnings of what the Lord intends to do. Let us pray, as Jesus taught us, that the Lord of the harvest might continue to stir the hearts of potential harvesters so that the great harvest he desires will be realized in our time.

CHAPTER 6:

Social Justice

S ocial justice is at the heart of the gospel message. When John's disciples asked Jesus if he was the messiah, he replied,

> The blind receive their sight, the lame walk, the lepers are cleansed and the deaf hear, and the dead are raised up, and the poor have good news preached to them (Matt. 11:5).

Our Lord himself validated his claim to messiahship in terms that included a ministry of social justice and liberation from the inequities of the human condition. Throughout the history of the church, social-justice ministry has continually had a major role to play in the spread of the gospel message. The care for the sick and for orphans, campaigns for the rights of the individual, reverence for the dead, educating the young, etc., are integral parts of the history of Christianity.

The social-justice ministry of the church today exists in continuity with the traditions of the past. The church still runs orphanages and hospitals. She still ministers to the

physical as well as spiritual needs of those in places where
she has a missionary outreach. She continues to educate not
only Catholic youth, but also other young persons who can
benefit from a Catholic educational environment, as in the
case of the late Cardinal Cody's inner-city Chicago parish
schools. Almost every parish, through the Legion of Mary,
St. Vincent de Paul, etc., has an ongoing ministry to the
needy.

However, in the past 100 years a new kind of social
teaching has begun to emerge from within the church.* This
teaching is designed to deal with some of the new aspects of
man's social problems that have surfaced as a result of
industrialization and the rise of technology. It focuses on
oppression and inequality, not only as manifested in individual lives, but also as they exist in an institutional way as
unfortunate byproducts of modern political and economic
situations. In this new setting, the Catholic has a new kind
of social-justice responsibility. He or she, in addition to
performing spiritual and corporal works of mercy for the
sake of individual persons (the traditional emphasis of Catholic social-justice teaching), must also find ways to counteract oppression and injustice on the institutional level. The
church's teaching in the area, proclaimed with increasing
insistence by all the popes since Leo XIII, has resulted in
Catholic involvement (especially lay involvement) in many
modern social-justice causes, such as labor unions, antiabor-
tion groups, women's-rights movements, campaigns against
racism, antiwar protests, antipoverty projects and fights
against political oppression.

Though the church has made great strides forward at the
level of church policy in confronting institutional social
injustice, the faithful are not yet fully equipped and capable
in the area. There exists in some circles an over-emphasis on
social justice to the detriment of the full gospel of eternal
salvation. This has been particularly true for many who are
involved in the work of liberation theology. Other Catholics,
especially those in more prosperous nations, are slow to
give up the material comfort and security their parents and

---

*Beginning with *Rerum Novarum*, Leo XIII's encyclical on labor in 1891.

grandparents gained for them in favor of a real commitment of time, energy and money for the cause of those oppressed by modern institutions.

The charismatic renewal so far has not taken the lead in fighting institutional oppression and injustice. In fact, most charismatics are still part of the problem. They are not yet equipped and willing to make substantial sacrifices of time, energy and money that are essential for effective social-justice ministry on the institutional level. There are some exceptions. The most notable is the work of Fr. Rick Thomas in his ministry to the poor of El Paso and Juarez,* but most of us must continue to open our hearts to the Lord so that his plan for institutional social action can be implemented at our grass-roots level.

Having acknowledged that more needs to be done by charismatics on the level of institutional social problems, I would like to discuss in this chapter how the renewal has, by ministering to the social problems of individuals, greatly enriched the lives of its participants. The typical charismatic prayer group, when viewed from the perspective of ministering to the sufferings, hurts and needs of individuals, can be correctly labeled, in my opinion, a "works of mercy" group. Though prayer groups are not usually set up to deal with personal and social suffering, the Lord normally leads many persons who hunger for this type of ministry to prayer meetings. As long as it is not made up of too many persons who themselves need "works of mercy" ministry, the group is able to offer some degree of help and consolation to almost all who ask for it. Prayer groups which are led by a strong core-group are often able to do much more.

Let us now consider how the Spirit uses the charismatic experience to enrich the lives of Catholics in the area of social justice under the aspect of performing the traditional works of mercy. There are 14 spiritual and corporal works of mercy. They are: to admonish the sinner, to instruct the ignorant, to counsel the doubtful, to comfort the sorrowful, to bear wrongs patiently, to forgive all injuries, to pray for

*See *Miracles in El Paso?*, by René Laurentin (Ann Arbor: Servant Publications, 1982).

the living and the dead, to feed the hungry, to give drink to the thirsty, to clothe the naked, to visit the imprisoned, to shelter the homeless, to visit the sick and to bury the dead.

Spiritual Works of Mercy

At first glance, one might think that the spiritual works of mercy are not really part of social-justice ministry. However, if a person recognizes that the root of all evil, including social problems, is sin and spiritual distress which the spiritual works of mercy are meant to address, then a person can correctly view these types of ministry as preventative social work. For example, alcoholism would certainly be classified as a social problem, but in charismatic experience this problem is often effectively dealt with by admonishing, praying with and counseling the alcoholic.

Admonish the Sinner

One grace given all of us in the renewal is a renewed sense of how evil and sinister sin is. The Lord also gives us a deeper and more spiritual love for one another. Thus, when we see brothers and sisters sinning against the Lord and one another, our love for them compels us to intervene and admonish them.

The most commonly experienced manifestation of this work of mercy in the renewal occurs in week four of the Life in the Spirit Seminar, during which participants are urged to examine themselves and to repent of whatever sins stand in the way of receiving the fullness of the Spirit. Through prayer rooms and the exercise of counselling gifts, this ministry becomes an ongoing part of the life of the prayer group.

I have personally experienced this work of mercy from both sides; that is, I have often been admonished effectively by brothers and sisters in Christ and, as a long-time member of a prayer-room team, I am often in the position of admonishing others. I praise God for mercifully pointing out my defects through those he sends to me. I can testify that the Lord has used me and others in the prayer room to admonish persons in ways that have had life-changing effects, including the overcoming of social problems such as alcoholism, drug abuse and marriage conflicts.

Instruct the Ignorant

This work of mercy, which refers not so much to offering general education to someone as it does to teaching and clarifying spiritual and doctrinal truths so that the individual can make progress in the Christian life, is a common ministry in charismatic circles. It is usually seen by those who benefit from it as one of the crucial ways the Spirit frees them from personal stress. The reason for this is that many problems Christians experience today come from having inadequate teaching on how practically to live Christian life, and the sound, clear, easy-to-understand teaching of the renewal on these matters is a welcome change from confused and misguided advice offered in many sectors of the church today.

I have made several breakthroughs in my Christian life after having been mercifully instructed out of my spiritual ignorance. Perhaps the most profound breakthrough involved a problem I had with fear. My life at one point was ruled in many ways by fear. Then I heard a talk on the subject entitled "Fear, Faith and Fight." My difficulties with fear were resolved almost immediately after I applied the instruction the Lord had mercifully given me through his people.

Counsel the Doubtful

Ministering to those who are unsure of what the Lord wants of them is a work of mercy that is made more real through the charismatic experience. Prior to being filled with the Spirit, we tended to approach decision-making with the assumption that it is very hard to know God's will, and that we have to make choices based mainly on reason and practical considerations. When we are filled with the

Spirit, the Lord gives us the gift of counsel (see chapter
two), through which we are able to know more clearly and
directly what his plan is for our lives. He also gives some of
us a special ability to counsel others. Whether we experience the spirit of counsel in its normal manifestation or as a
special charism, this gift enables us to counsel the doubtful
with a spiritual power that we would not have otherwise.

This work of mercy is often performed when praying with
people about a decision that must be made. We might pray
for a passage on the matter, receive a word from the Lord,
get a vision or mental image, or simply have some sound,
prudent advice to offer. However it is ministered, charismatic counseling greatly increases a person's ability to make
decisions that bear fruit in the Lord. The mentality of contemporary society, which tends to throw everything into
doubt, makes the counseling of the doubtful all the more
crucial to fostering successful life in the Spirit. This is
especially true with regard to those whose work, family and
emotional lives are in a state of disarray.

Comfort the Sorrowful

Ours is an age in which sorrow is experienced as much as
in other times, but this experience is too often hidden or
covered over by pleasure-seeking and materialistic escapism.
The Lord seems to use the typical prayer meeting to un-
cover many of the hidden and suppressed sorrows we feel.
Often, through prophetic words and scripture readings, the
Lord will speak to us of our sorrow and call on us to cling to
him as our comfort. As we respond to this word, admitting
to the Lord and to ourselves our sadness at the difficulty of
our lives and calling on him to be our consolation, we
experience peace and joy in the Holy Spirit.

The fellowship in the Lord which gradually develops as
charismatic groups grow also provides consolation from our
sorrows. Just sharing our difficulties with a friend in Christ
and experiencing his or her sympathy provides an enormous amount of comfort. Burdens due to problems such as
emotional distress, family difficulties, joblessness, illness,

death of a loved one, etc., are lessened a little simply by sharing them with one another in the group.

Bear Wrongs Patiently, Forgive All Injuries

In chapter three, I spoke of how the charismatic experience enriched my ability to seek and give forgiveness. Another dimension of the area of reconciliation that life in the Spirit enriches involves forbearance. Often, though we may have forgiven persons who wronged us, they may not want to repent of their sins against us, or they may not even be aware of having injured us. In these cases, we must make sure that we do not harbor vengefulness and enmity against them in our hearts. Also, if they continue to treat us wrongly, or do something that causes us prolonged suffering, we must practice forbearance in the Lord.

In the renewal, these works of mercy, which are performed mainly inside of us (though they do affect the way we relate to those who have injured us) are fostered by teaching on the subject and through prayer sessions, such as prayers for inner healing and the healing of memories. In charismatic teaching, the points mentioned above about keeping our hearts in a forgiving mode are emphasized. In prayer sessions, persons are urged to let the Lord show them how bitterness, resentment, lack of forgiveness or vengefulness have gotten in the way of relating in a fully open and loving way to others. Such sessions are often seen by those who participate in them as breakthrough events in their lives.

Pray for the Living and the Dead

At a time when many misguided Catholic thinkers are questioning the power of intercessory prayer, the Lord has manifested its great power and effectiveness through the charismatic experience. Who among us has not many times prayed for the living and seen the Lord respond to those prayers in a way that he would not have responded had we not asked? We may have interceded for physical healing, for spiritual healing, for a situation at work or in the home, for God to intervene providentially in some event, or for any other need that our Father would want to fill for us. Who among us, after praying for the dead, has not experienced the spiritual sense that the Lord has heard our prayer and that it is effective in bringing one person more quickly into eternal bliss?

Intercessory prayer for both the living and the souls in purgatory is the most powerful of all works of mercy. Through it, we do not act ourselves, but we enable God himself to move in people's lives directly in ways that, for his own reasons, he will not move without our prayer participation. Though charismatics are not the only Christians today who regularly practice this work of mercy, the Lord has enriched the experience of it in charismatic life by responding regularly to Spirit-filled prayers of intercession in extraordinary ways.

The Corporal Works of Mercy

Having considered the charismatic "preventative" ministry of social justice in people's spiritual lives, let us now turn to a discussion of how the renewal is used by the Lord to meet the material and physical needs of those who come in contact with it.

Feed the Hungry; Clothe the Naked; Give Drink to the Thirsty; Shelter the Homeless

Most prayer groups perform these works of mercy at least to some degree for the simple reason that people in need continually go to charismatic meetings and ask for help. On one side of the spectrum, one can point to the work of Fr. Rick Thomas, whom we have already mentioned. His extraordinary level of ministry to the physical needs of the poor is found in only a few other groups, though this type of ministry could become more common in the future. More typical is the case of the small prayer group that is not set up to care for physical needs, but responds with what little resources it has when persons in various states of need come to it for help. A person may only get a meal, some clothes, some money, or a bed for a weekend, but even this little work of mercy does not go unnoticed by the Lord. As Christ taught, "Whosoever gives to one of these little ones even a cup of cold water because he is a disciple, truly I say to you, he will not lose his reward" (Mt. 10:42).

Some groups organize themselves so that they are able to do more. This is the case with my community. Over the years we have developed a system of offering hospitality, feeding and clothing those who seek us out, and even offering long-term social ministry to those with special needs. I lived in a house that took in an alcoholic for three months, cared for an emotionally disturbed man for two years, and provided a halfway house for a former drug pusher for two years.

Charismatics are not alone among Catholics today in performing these corporal works of mercy, but they are specially blessed because in their groups everyone has an opportunity to have a real and active role in helping those who have these needs. In a normal parish setting, an active level of ministry is typically the task (and privilege) of the few who have time and resources to go to those in need, while others can offer only moral and financial support.

Visit Prisoners

Charismatics often develop fruitful prison ministries. Here is a sharing from a friend who has an active prison ministry.

"Men in prison entered my life some years ago and led me to believe that visiting prisoners was a work that God was calling me to. The paradox struck me at the time—a call to enter more fully into life in the Spirit meant a call to enter the gates of the state penitentiary.

"For the past three years, I have been visiting prisoners at a nearby prison on a monthly basis. I really enjoy the 45-minute drive to the prison, sharing and joking with the other men who go with me to visit the prisoners. But, as we near our destination, our conversation tapers off. No matter how many times you've been there, there's always a chill as you turn the corner and catch first sight of that massive mound of concrete.

"Guards search us and lead us through a series of locked gates into the large visiting room. The prisoners come in one by one, each wearing a name tag and ID photo. It's the only way an outsider could tell us apart.

"We talk together in a group and then pair off one to one. It's not that much different from talking to a neighbor or a coworker. You find common ground. But being filled with the Spirit gives one a greater sensitivity to where our brothers or sisters are in their lives and makes our conversations richer and more fruitful, even though they might not be about spiritual or religious matters.

"After an hour or so, it's time to leave. There are handshakes and 'See you next month.' Now the hard part. We leave the visiting room by different doors. One door leads to the crisp night air, and the other one leads back to the cellblock with 1,500 other men. I often think—but for the grace of God, I could be leaving by the other door.

"I believe that the Lord has used me through the power of his Spirit to enrich in some small way the difficult lives of the men I have come to know in prison. But, much more significantly, he has used my prison ministry to enrich my own life. He has taught me that he is most visible in the persons of those the world considers most invisible—the poor, the aged, the prisoners. I have come to know that I don't bring him with me into prison and take him out when I leave (though, in as far as I am his servant, I do bring his love into prisons); I find him there in the men I visit. They are Christ to me in a deeper way than I am Christ to them. I am increasingly led to believe that, since God loves me with a merciful love that does not depend on what I have done, I must also have that same love for prisoners—and everyone else—loving them in a merciful, nonjudgmental way no matter what."

Visit the Sick

Charismatic ministry to the sick is so powerful and broad in scope that it is not necessary to offer examples of how it enriches the lives of Catholic charismatics. Visiting, praying

with, consoling, interceding and caring for the sick are by
far the most popular works of mercy practiced in the charismatic renewal. It is also the charismatic ministry that has
had the most substantial impact on the church at large.

Bury the Dead

Ten members of my charismatic group have died over the
years. The mercy and compassion with which their friends
and loved ones are treated by the group has always been
inspiring. But even more striking is the great hope that is
always present at charismatic funerals. The baptism in the
Spirit spiritualizes our life-perspective. This spiritualization
produces, among other things, a change in our perspective
toward eternity. As we grow in the Spirit, heaven and spending eternity with our Lord become increasingly our main
hope in life. So, when we witness the death of a brother or
sister in the Lord who has shared that hope, we feel a deep
sense of joy because we know in faith that a member of
Christ's body has just ended his or her life on earth and has
reached the goal that we all long for. When this deep and
abiding belief is added to the charismatic ability to express
outwardly sentiments of joy and sorrow, the celebration of
the passing of a loved one from this life to eternal life
becomes a rich and profoundly moving experience for all
who participate in it.

The Future of Social Justice Among Charismatics

Many have spoken of the great potential that exists in the
charismatic renewal for effective labor in the area of social
justice. We have so far considered the weakness of the
renewal on the level of dealing with institutional social ills
and its strength in the area of individual ills. How can we
charismatics grow in our social-justice lives in a way that
maintains our ability to minister to the individual while
more effectively addressing the institutional ills that the
Spirit has been calling on the whole church to address for at

least the past 100 years? The beginnings of the answer to this question can be found in the social-justice ministry of some of the stronger groups that exist in America. These groups, because of their organizational ability, the maturity of their members and their level of commitment, are able to do much more than the normal prayer group for individuals who come to them for help.

I believe that the Lord wants to draw all participants in the renewal to greater social awareness and activity by using these groups as models. A number of groups of this type exist across the country. Some of them are covenant communities; others are not. They need to be studied and learned from by the wider renewal. When this is done, we will more clearly see the Lord's plan for using life in the Spirit to minister to the poor and suffering in our midst.

The rest of this chapter will be devoted to explaining the social-justice ministry of one of these groups, my community, the People of Praise in South Bend, Indiana. Over the years, the Lord has constructed in my community a successful method for dealing with social ills. The explanation that follows will, I hope, offer readers an enriched vision of how they can work to minister social justice more effectively in their groups.

Social Justice and the People of Praise

The People of Praise has, from its inception, always been committed to an active ministry in the area of social justice. We have evolved a method of social action which has been quite effective in dealing with the social and personal problems of hundreds of persons who have come to us for help. The key principle of our method of social action is that we use a total environment in ministering to the needs of those whom we are helping. We deal with problems by having people move into the community environment, where they can be cared for 24 hours a day, 7 days a week. We try to tailor the specific environment and relationships to their particular needs. Thus, for example, if an emotionally disturbed person came to us for help, we would place him or her in a strong, stable, family environment, in which those caring for him or her would have had some prior experience in dealing with this type of problem. An alcoholic might live in a situation where he could dry out for a while and then be moved to other situations where he could receive different kinds of ongoing help from persons in the community who were skilled in other areas of need.

We have chosen the environmental approach rather than the functional approach because it seems to work better. We feel that the functional approach, although certainly not without merit, cannot effectively deal with the complex problems that most people face, and also does not bring to bear enough resources to overcome the enormous obstacles which people are confronting. For example, take the case of an unwed mother whom the government is trying to help. A functionally oriented group may give her money to live on. They may give her counseling to help her if she has emotional problems. They may offer daycare so that she can work to support her family. But this is just the beginning of her problem. What about her personal loneliness? What about possible rejection from family and society? Who will replace the father in helping her raise her children? And so on. Our community has done all these things and more for a number of unwed mothers, and we have done it through an environmental approach.

Another aspect of our social work is that we aim for total recovery for the person we are helping. We try to solve not only the specific problem that a person might have, but try also to get his or her whole life moving toward integration. We believe that specific problems are usually a symptom of deeper, more substantial difficulties, and that, if we really want to bring about substantial progress, then we have to minister to the whole person. Thus, for example, if we are trying to help an alcoholic, we would also minister to his job situation, family life, etc.

We also would describe ourselves as working on a nonmedical model when we help others. In other words, we do not look upon those we help as sick or as "cases," but as brothers and sisters in Christ who need our services. We feel that, although the medical model is effective in many situations, it does not fit an environmentally oriented ministry such as ours.

One aspect of our method which is perhaps unique is our ability to handle a wide variety of problems. This flexibility has developed over the years in response to the wide variety of problems that we encountered. Different people came to us with different problems, and some people came to us, each of whom had a whole set of problems. Being located in many houses around the city, we were able to analyze different living situations and guide people into the ones which would be most helpful. Gradually, we have developed the capability to deal with almost every kind of social difficulty common in our society.

Our approach also gives each member of the community an opportunity to be directly involved in working for social justice in practical, concrete ways. The most a person can normally do in our culture is to give money to some agency which sponsors the work being done. Our method allows for active participation on the part of all. This has two advantages. First, it brings more energy to bear on the problems being dealt with. Second, the lives of the members of the group are greatly enriched through the sacrifices they make in their work.

Some persons view us from the outside as having no social-justice orientation. This is because our approach is environmental and, therefore, is not as easily recognizable as most social-action programs, which are functionally oriented. Also, we do not advertize what we do. We feel that, since the people we are ministering to are brothers and sisters in Christ, it would be wrong to encourage the view that they are projects we have successfully completed.

Using the above approach, our community has ministered to the social justice needs of over 200 persons in the past few years. We have ministered to a broad variety of difficulties, from alcoholism, drug abuse and mental disorders, to poverty, Far Eastern refugees, broken marriages, unwed mothers, and children with only one parent. Our ministry has involved all aspects of the lives of those who came to us in need. We are grateful to the Lord for giving us the privilege of caring for so many of his little ones.

CHAPTER 7:

The Twelve *Rhemas*

Thus far we have attempted to clarify the meaning of the charismatic renewal by discussing how it can be explained in terms of aspects of Catholic life which are outside itself, so to speak. Vatican II, Catholic spirituality, sacramental life, parish life, Catholic evangelism and social justice (along with Catholic scriptural consciousness and Marian piety) are ways of thinking about one's life as a Catholic which exist on their own, outside the charismatic experience. It is helpful for us in the renewal to be able to understand our experience according to the terminology of these standpoints because, in doing so, we will arrive at a more balanced and fully Catholic vision of our life in the Spirit.

But it would also be helpful for us to clarify for ourselves the meaning of the charismatic renewal from the "inside." What is the essence of the life in the Spirit when viewed without reference to other aspects of the Catholic mentality? What would an experience-based explanation of charismatic life look like?

Charismatics usually answer this question by offering spiritual histories of the renewal. These histories recount the

unfolding of charismatic life in terms of different aspects of
Christian life that the Lord seemed to emphasize at different
points in the renewal's history. For example, Fr. Mike Scanlon
has spoken of the movement moving from a time of blessing to one of testing and judgment. Fr. George Kosicki talks
of us going from the glory of Tabor to the suffering of
Calvary and on to the victory of the Resurrection and
Pentecost. Others have offered similar visions and, in my
opinion, all are in the Spirit and accurately describe what
the Lord is doing.

There is a common thread which runs through most of the
current visions of the meaning of the renewal from the inside.
The thread is that we are a dynamic, pilgrim people being led
through the wilderness of the modern world by the word of
the Lord as it is spoken in "now words" of prophecy, teaching,
discernment, counsel and wisdom. These "now words," by
which we mean the dominant themes in the renewal at certain
points in its history, are usually referred to as *rhemas* in
charismatic circles. (According to some scholars, *rhema* is New
Testament Greek for the spoken word, as opposed to *logos*,
which means the written word of scripture.)

I would like to offer an account of the spiritual history of
the renewal in terms of 12 key "now words," or *rhemas*,
which I believe the Lord has been speaking to his charismatic people over the last 16 years. I will consider each *rhema*
as it appeared during the spiritual-historical unfolding of
the renewal. I will try to show how the *rhemas* followed one
another and built upon one another. By the time we come
to the end of our analysis, we will, I hope, have a deeper
understanding of who we are and where we are going
"from the inside," that is, in terms of our own experience.
The 12 *rhemas* are: in the Spirit, charisms, involvement,
commitment, relationships, authority, sexuality, family, the
cross, back to basics, integration and the age of evangelism.

In the Spirit

Before the advent of the renewal in the mid-60s, very few
Catholics were able to relate positively to scriptural phrases

such as "full of the Spirit," "in the Spirit," "baptized with the Spirit," all of which are a common part of the vocabulary of our Pentecostal brethren. We viewed Pentecostals and their style of Christianity as unbalanced, emotionalistic and somewhat bizarre. During the years when Vatican II was in session, however, the Spirit began to put in the hearts of many Catholics a hunger for "something more." He used the council and such movements as the *Cursillo*, the liturgical movement and the Christian Family Movement to stir up this hunger. In his personal testimony, Kevin Ranaghan, one of the founders of the renewal, used to say that, though he faithfully tried to implement the council in his life, worked in the *Cursillo* and campaigned hard for liturgical renewal, there was a void in his soul. "I knew," he said, "that there *had* to be something more." He was like many dedicated Catholics, then and now.

Then, under the impulse of the Spirit, our Pentecostal brothers and sisters began to pray with us for the baptism in the Spirit, and the charismatic renewal began. Our hunger for something more was being satisfied, not by a new idea or program, but by the Lord himself. Those who experienced this baptism could now relate to phrases such as "in the Spirit," and to the whole style of emotional, biblically oriented, experiential Christianity that these phrases describe.

Today, being in the Spirit stands as the initial *rhema* which a person hears in his heart when he is prayed with. For those of us who have gone on to appropriate other *rhemas* as the Lord leads us on, being in the Spirit still remains the foundation of our charismatic lives in a profound way.

The Charisms

Following quickly on the heels of the in-the-Spirit *rhema* was a call from the Lord to appropriate and use the different charisms mentioned in the New Testament. When people were baptized in the Spirit, gifts of tongues, prophecy, miracles, healing and discernment immediately surfaced. In part, this happened because the Christian lives of the Pentecostals who prayed with us included such manifestations. The outbreak of the charisms can also be traced to the love for scripture, which is a normal result of the baptism in the Spirit. When we were filled with the Spirit, we were drawn to the New Testament for an explanation of what was happening, and the apostolic testimony often points to charismatic activity as an immediate result of receiving the Spirit. A third reason for the outbreak of the charisms was that they fulfilled a need for order felt by those who first became involved. The baptism in the Spirit was great, but people did not know what to do next. How were they to put some kind of structure into their new lives? The *rhema* of the charisms gave them something more concrete to work with.

The *rhema* of the charisms has gone through a great deal of development and clarification since it was first spoken. Healing and prophecy have been manifest with great power as healers such as Francis MacNutt, Fr. Diorio, and Fr. Ed McDonnough and prophets such as Ralph Martin and Kevin Ranaghan have ministered nationally. Tongues has proven to be an invaluable part of life in the Spirit. More charisms have been added to the initial list of tongues, miracles, healing, prophecy and discernment. Insight and understanding of how a person's function in the body of Christ is discerned and developed have grown and continue to grow. Each of us, as we enter the renewal, has a much greater wealth of experience to draw on than did those who pioneered this area. But the basic *rhema* remains as a foundation for life in the Spirit; when the Lord fills us with his Spirit, he gives each different gifts for the common good.

Involvement

A strong fellowship among prayer-group members was part of charismatic life from the first days. It fulfilled the obvious need for talking about and sorting out the various aspects of the new life that had been found. In addition, since the baptism in the Spirit caused one to become, in many ways, a different person, and thus usually caused some alienation from old friends who sensed that we were "just not the same anymore," fellowship provided the opportunity for the making of new friends and acquaintances with the fullness of the Spirit as the unifying factor.

But the *rhema* of involvement did not appear strongly for a while. Many, after a year or so of having prayer meetings, using the charisms, etc., began to refocus their lives on ways of being Catholic which they formerly practiced. (One might say that this was the first example of the so-called revolving door tendency.) Some went back to *Cursillo*; others to parish renewal; others to liturgical renewal. Their prayer-meeting acquaintances began to seem unlikely associates for long-term Christian friendship. It was at this point that the Lord began to speak in prophecy about the need for community. He kept saying that *he* had brought us together, and that *he* had a plan, and that we should continue to follow his leadings. We sensed that he wanted us to form core groups, to meet on a night other than the prayer-meeting night to organize the meeting and to see what else he might say to the newly formed core groups. He also began to tell us that we should begin to love one another in more real ways. He said that we needed to involve ourselves with one another, not for one or two nights a week, but in a deeper way so that we could meet more of one another's real needs.

This stage in the history of the renewal, during which the Lord led us on from prayer together and loose association to involvement in one another's lives and problems, constitutes the third *rhema*. It continues today to be a key step for the prayer group. The Lord loves our worship and charisms, but his plan is for our whole lives to be transformed. This cannot happen in isolation. We need to become involved wih one another to move forward in becoming a more effective manifestation of the body of Christ.

Commitment

The *rhema* of involvement of lives with one another seemed at first to create more problems than it solved. As we involved ourselves more with one another and as our personal lives were brought more into the light, it seemed increasingly clear that we had a lot of problems. These problems were much greater and more difficult to solve than we had imagined.

Our greatest difficulty, we gradually realized, was that none of us seemed to be able to spend the time and energy that it would take to solve our life problems. People would come together sometimes, but other times they would have something else to do. Some would quit the group altogether and perhaps move to another place. Few seemed eager to follow good advice when it was given. The Lord had led us into a spiritual place that seemed to call for some further leading in order to bear fruit. This led us into the next *rhema*, that of commitment of our lives to one another.

The *rhema* of commitment has had several major effects on charismatic life. First, it opened the way to solving the life problems which anything less than committed relating could not solve. We found that, if we were seriously committed to helping one another work through obstacles to Christian maturity, both in terms of sticking with the situation and in terms of listening to good advice, the Lord would bless our efforts. Second, it "nailed the revolving door shut," so to speak, and effectively overcame our temptations to quit or give up the path of Spirit-filled life. Third, it allowed the charismatic renewal to continue. The renewal is a great work of God in our time but, without a heart-commitment to it, we would have quickly found other good things with which to occupy our time, and gradually the broad work of the Spirit would have withered. Fourth, it was crucial to growth in charity. The Lord himself is a committed covenant-lover who makes promises and keeps them. If we were to be remade into his image in love by the power of the Spirit, then we, like him, had to structure our lives of charity such that they included committed relationships with other Christians.

This *rhema* led to the formation of the 100 or so covenant communities that exist today. It also led many other prayer groups and prayer communities to make solid commitments among themselves, which, though not as intense or full as the committedness of covenant communities, still have allowed for a great enriching of life in the Spirit, especially in terms of commitment to one's parish.

Relationships

The way commitment led into relationships was similar to the way in the Spirit led into charisms. Commitment produced a sense of beginning to embark on a new way of living, and one sensed a new bond with those who had also made commitments. The scripture seemed suddenly to be teeming with instruction about how to live a life of committed love. All experienced the need to begin to put some order in this new way of living.

Much of the initial direction for the *rhema* of relationships came from Steve Clark. Clark, an important teacher in the early history of the renewal, taught convincingly about *agape* love as committed, self-sacrificing love, and not a love based on feelings. He insisted on the need for active, ongoing forgiveness in daily life. He clarified the distinction between worldly relationships and those in which Christ was the center. He pointed to the need for solid and active guidance in one's life in the Spirit.

The *rhema* of relationships is not yet completed. Since the time of Clark's initial teaching on the matter, more good teaching has been given. But Clark's initial insights on commitment, reconciliation, worldly relationships and guidance are still foundational words that the Lord uses to get us started when we appropriate the *rhema* of relationships.

Authority

Although there were leaders in the charismatic renewal from the beginning, it was only with great caution that the Lord imparted his word on authority to us. This is due to the negative view of authority held by modern man. I remember at one of our meetings in 1967 that we had a strong disagreement on whether there should be a leader of the prayer meeting. We mistakenly decided that we should let the Spirit lead, and have no human leader.

As time went on and we began to do more, we did accept some as leaders, but it was not until 1974 that the Lord really came forth with a strong *rhema* on the real, positive value of authority. He said that authority was not bad, and that even the Son was under the Father's authority. He said that authority can bring about a greater unity among his people, enabling them to do more for his kingdom. He said that he was raising up some to be in authority, and that, if we trusted him to bless those he was raising up and followed their lead, good fruit would grow.

The *rhema* of authority is still being sorted out in the renewal. Though it has produced some unfortunate side-effects, it has proven to be a key *rhema* in our wilderness journey as a charismatic pilgrim people. On a small scale, it has enabled covenant communities to move forward more strongly than before. On the level of the broader renewal, it has enabled those involved in parish renewal to listen more closely to their lay leaders, priests and bishops.

Sexuality

Beneath much of the personal turmoil that eventually surfaced in the lives of some who were filled with the Spirit was a profoundly disordered sexual life. The Lord ministered to this problem by offering Spirit-filled persons clear teaching and direction on how to live as the men and women God made us to be.

The sexuality *rhema* has arisen mainly out of the experience of the covenant communities. This is the case because sexuality is a profoundly complex issue, and it is difficult to address it outside of a situation which provides a sufficiently strong environment to deal with its complexity. However, the insights that come from the covenant communities can be applied by anyone filled with the Spirit.

The first part of the *rhema* is that the Lord wants us to be brothers and sisters to one another and fight the modern temptation to see one another mainly as objects of our desire. The second part is that sexual sin can be overcome, no matter how deeply it seems to be ingrained in our character. The third part is that we should not see the God-given differences between us as men or women as a problem, but should glorify the Lord that he has made us men and women, in his image, and seek ways to enhance our masculinity or feminity in the Lord.

The Family

The *rhema* on family has unfolded slowly in the course of the renewal. At first, most participants saw life in the Spirit as something mainly for adults. The movements they had been involved in previously, such as the *Cursillo* and the liturgical movement, were directed toward giving adult Catholics a way to help renew the church. Also, many participants were unmarried students and young adults who had no direct concern for family life.

Gradually, the first participants in the renewal shared more and more of their lives, including their family lives, while the young unmarried persons got married and began to raise their families. Thus, concern for family life increased. Also, there was a point in the history of the renewal, in the early 70s, when the charismatic movement became less attractive to the young, searching idealists who first got it started, and more attractive to normal Catholics who, among other things, were trying to keep their families intact in the modern world.

There is another, more spiritual reason behind the gradual manner in which the family *rhema* developed. The *rhema* immediately preceding family was sexuality. To prepare his pilgrim people for renewed family life, the Lord first gave them a fresh vision of Christian sexuality. The *rhema* which preceded sexuality, that of authority, also was needed as a foundation on which authority in family life could be built. The two which preceded this *rhema*—relationship and commitment—are even more basic as foundations for living successful family life in the Spirit. My point here is that, before the family *rhema* could be imparted, the Lord had to do a lot of groundwork with regard to areas of life in the Spirit which, though not applicable only to family life, are the key spiritual building blocks of successful family life. With these *rhemas* in place, the Lord was able to speak his word on family effectively.

The content of the family *rhema* runs basically as follows. The Lord, who himself is a family, has called his sons and daughters to live their lives as families in his image and likeness. He wants to raise up strong families as the foundation for his renewed body in the future. With their permanent covenant as a foundation, loving one another first as brother and sister, properly understanding the role of authority and submission in marriage, and living out their sexual lives in Christ, the Lord is calling husbands and wives to save their families. He is calling them actively to train their children in the faith, and not to leave them at the mercy of the lies of secular society. He is calling them to set up an alternate society within the family to protect it from current attacks on faith in most areas of contemporary life. He is calling on families in the Spirit to band together with other families in the Spirit so that there can be added support and protection in this great work of family restoration.

The Cross

As these *rhemas* unfolded, the Lord would, from time to time, call us all to remain centered in the central mystery of our faith, that is, the cross. But, beginning with the year following the ecumenical gathering in Kansas City in 1977, the call to the cross began to intensify. Many prophetic voices spoke of the end of a time of blessings and gifts and of the beginning of a time of judgment and testing.

The *rhema* of the cross reached its full expression at the 1981 national conference, where the theme was the power of the cross. Who among those of us who attended that conference can forget the striking scene of the large cross of St. Francis of Assisi which was suspended over the speakers' platform? Who will forget the exhortations from Babsy

Bleasdell, Ern Baxter and the other speakers that we embrace the cross as the way to victory?

What was the purpose of this *rhema*? Why did it surface at the time it did? I believe that the cross was a watershed or transitional *rhema* in our pilgrim journey. It came after we had been given a full vision of the living out of Spirit-filled life on the level of our behavior—one might call it the horizontal level. We had been led by the Lord through a process of recovering the Christian vision of society and civilization, from the emotional and behavioral life of the individual, on to life in the family and group, and on to the life of the body of Christ. The next step, it might seem, ought to be bringing our insights from the Lord into integration with the rest of his body, i.e., the church.

But the Lord knew that we were not ready for such a step. We needed to grow vertically first. We needed to grow in spiritual depth as well as breadth. We needed sanctification as well as civilization. We needed to become humble and purified before we could offer our particular part in God's renewing of his church to our brothers and sisters in the universal church. And so, the Lord began to teach us in a more intense way about the meaning of his cross in our lives.

As this *rhema* was being spoken, many retreated from active involvement in the renewal. The phenomenal numerical growth of the movement slowed down. Those who remained, accustomed to the time of blessing we had enjoyed for so long, flinched at the onset of the time of testing and purification. The prophetic exhortation of Fr. John Bertolucci that we "hang in there" began to hit home as the difficult way of Calvary opened up before us. As we have endured this time, the difficulty of our lives has been diminished by our growing sense of the power and glory of his cross.

Back to Basics

The next *rhema* to be spoken by the Lord, that of returning to the spiritual roots of our charismatic life—back to basics—is beginning to emerge today. The cross *rhema* which preceded it has as one of its purposes preparing us for the *rhema* of integration, but the cross also leads us back to refocusing our lives on the thirst for deeper union with God which constituted the original impulse for the renewal.

The Lord is calling us back to the love which we sought and received at first. But we are not being called to do this as merely a revival of what happened in the beginning. He has taught us much since we first experienced his Spirit, and our return to the basics must be one which involves a more mature and enduring appropriation of life in him, taking into account all that he has taught us in the past.

Although there are many signs of the emergence of the back-to-basics *rhema*, it remains to be seen what this "now word" from the Lord will look like when it is fully developed.

Integration

Regarding this *rhema* one might ask, "Hasn't this kind of thing—that is, integrating the renewal into the whole church—been going on all along?" Viewed from one perspective, this is certainly the case. Much of the early literature and teaching of the renewal was concerned with the need for integration. Clark's *Baptism in the Spirit and Confirmation* and Ranaghan's *The Lord, the Spirit and the Church* are two well-known examples of this. All through the history of the renewal, integration has been an important priority of both its leaders and its participants.

On the level of the whole church, Cardinal Suenens, by means of his many books and speeches, through his *Malines Documents*, and through his role as patron of the renewal, has contributed much. The Rome conference of 1975 was a significant instance of progress toward integration on the international level, as have been the several subsequent meetings between John Paul II and various charismatic leaders. On the diocesan level, many bishops and priests have faithfully shepherded prayer groups in this direction.

However, the integrations that have taken place so far have involved only parts of the full word that the Lord has spoken to the renewal. The charismatic experience in its fullness—which I have labelled the 12 *rhemas*—has yet to be integrated.

What will full integration look like? Will it mean that the time has come for the renewal to "die" and "lose itself" in the broader church, as happened in the case of the liturgical movement? (Many leaders have suggested this.) Ought it to become an officially recognized society within the church, complete with rules, structures, membership, etc.? Or has it simply run its course, and should we all go on now to the next movement? No, this is not the meaning of the *rhema* of integration.

The new *rhema* means that all the words the Lord has delivered to us in previous years must be spoken by us to the church as we remain strong and intact as a movement. We cannot cease to be who we are just so that we can talk to others about it. We cannot, for example, get fired up by the baptism in the Spirit to renew our parishes and then abandon our charismatic life later on in favor of parish renewal because it is "more important," as so many have done. There is a dying involved in integration, but it is not the dying of the movement itself. It is a dying which was spoken of in the cross *rhema*—a dying to our selfishness, longing for comfort and inward focus—a dying to our tendency to avoid the suffering and difficulty which we encounter as we carry our message to those who find it hard to accept and understand what we say. It is a dying which the back-to-basics *rhema* is preparing us for by reestablishing us, in a sounder and more mature way, on the foundation of our early experience.

This book is an attempt at integration. Through it, I have tried to offer self-understanding to charismatics, both with regard to their Catholic-ness and their Spirit-filled-ness. Such understanding can give us a way to move toward greater harmony with the whole church, while enabling us to maintain ourselves in our enriched charismatic life.

I do not know what the *rhema* of integration will look like when it has fully emerged. It is for this reason that I have offered only a basic guideline to follow—seek fuller harmony but don't lose one's identity. When integration reaches its fullness, we will be ready for the final *rhema* in this spiritual history, which is the coming age of evangelism.

Age of Evangelism

Evangelism has, of course, been at the heart of the renewal since it began. The famous Duquesne weekend of
early 1967, which is generally recognized as the historical
starting point of the renewal, was a *Cursillo*-style weekend
retreat which was designed to evangelize its participants.
From that point on, evangelism has continually been a major call and concern of all participants in the renewal.

But there has lately been talk among some in the renewal
of a time of evangelism on a much broader scale. Many see
the eventual fruit of the past and present suffering and
purification of the church as a preparation for this coming
time. I will not now elaborate on this still-future *rhema*. I
mention it in my vision of the renewal because it has been a
consistent prophetic word in some circles for the past few
years, and because it seems "in the Spirit" that a fitting
completion to our charismatic wandering in the desert of
the modern world would be to make the desert bloom
through the outpouring of the living waters of the Holy
Spirit of God.

Come, Holy Spirit!